REALM OF WEALTH

The 9 Cycles of Prosperity

by
James Tavian Alexander

REALM OF WEALTH

The 9 Cycles of Prosperity

by
James Tavian Alexander

Rhino Publishing, S.A.
www.RhinoPublishing.net
Republic of Panama

REALM OF WEALTH
The 9 Cycles of Prosperity

Copyright © 2007 by James Tavian Alexander
All rights reserved.

This edition is published by Rhino Publishing.
For information, contact Christian Martin Desharnais
through Rhino Publishing website, www.RhinoPublishing.net

Published in the Republic of Panama.

Without limiting the rights under copyright reserved above, no part of this book may be reproduced, stored in or introduced into a retrieval system, or transmitted, in any form or by any means (electronic, mechanical, photocopying, recording, or otherwise), without permission in writing from both the copyright owner and the publisher, except by reviewer who may quote brief passages in a review.

ISBN: 978-9962-636-72-4

RHINO PUBLISHING, S.A.
www.rhinopublishing.net
World Trade Center
Panama, 00832-2483
Republic of Panama

Go to www.9cycles.info and download your free copy of your Realm of Wealth workbook so you've got it in your hands before you begin your journey.

CONTENTS

Pages

AUTHOR'S NOTE	xi
INTRODUCTION	xv

CHAPTER 1
CYCLE OF RECIPROCITY:

YOU GET AFTER YOU GIVE	1
How the Ancients discovered the Cycle	1
Tithing	2
Reverse Tithing	6
Honor Yourself	8
Compensation	9

CHAPTER 2

CYCLE OF COMMAND	13
How to Amplify and Accelerate your Desires	13
Affirmations and the Cycle of Command	14
Getting that Z4	18

CHAPTER 3

CYCLE OF ATTRACTION	21
Like Attracts Like	21
Are we the Attractor or the Attracted?	22
Making it Happen	24
Steps to Accelerate the Cycle of Attraction	29
Personal Magnetism	30

CHAPTER 4

VACUUM CYCLE OF PROSPERITY	33
How You could be Preventing Prosperity in Your Life	33

	Pages
Mental Spring Cleaning	34
The Psychology of Good Clothes	38
Creative Plans to Achieve your Goals	45
Desires to Goals	47

CHAPTER 5:
CYCLE OF IMAGINATION 53
   The Top Sure-Fire Technique to Supercharge
      Your Prosperity 53
   Activating the Cycle of Imagination 55

CHAPTER 6
CYCLE OF INCREASE 59
   Leveraging the Prosperity Equation 59
   The Magic of Praise 60
   Increasing the Power of the Cycle of Increase 63

CHAPTER 7
CYCLE OF CONCENTRATION 67
   Developing a Single-Mindedness to Abundance 67
   How to establish the Cycle of Concentration 68
   Persistence 74

CHAPTER 8
THE WEALTH MINDSET CYCLE 81
   The crucial element in attracting abundance 81
   Poverty Consciousness versus Prosperity
      Consciousness 84
   The Age of Abundance 91

CHAPTER 9
THE CYCLE OF INTUITION 93
   Your Mastermind Force for Prosperity 93
   Types of Intuition 94

Pages

BONUS CHAPTER ONE
The Essential Strengths of Self-Confidence
& Self-Esteem 99
 Self-Esteem Evaluation 101
 Positive Affirmations 102
 I am: A statement personal identity 103
 I can: A declaration of your potential 103
 I will: A statement of positive change in your life 104
 Self-Nurturing 106
 Praise 108

BONUS CHAPTER TWO
Revolutionize your Health with the
Cycles of Prosperity 111
 Living the Cyclonic Life 117
 Working in the Information Age 120

BONUS CHAPTER THREE
How to Maintain your Mental Efficiency 125

A FINAL WORD 129

AUTHOR'S NOTE

The study of natural cyclic events is called phenology. In its simplest terms, phenology is the study of the life cycles of plants and animals. Cycles are found in all areas of life, from the tiniest cell to the limitless cosmos. From single-celled organisms to plants, and from the climatic cycles to galaxies, much of what we know is governed and influenced by cycles.

Many years ago, when I was 16 years old, I read a book called <u>Think and Grow Rich</u>, by Napoleon Hill – this book changed my life and led me to a lifelong interest in personal development, success achievement, and a desire to understand the fundamentals of profound change. After many years of research and practical experimentation, I am ready to share what I have learned. Sharing my discoveries will begin to complete the cycle, for what I have learned was passed to me with the understanding that it would be made available to others as well.

Since reading Napoleon Hill's classic, I have used these universal truths, these laws, or what I have determined to be *Cycles*, in my own life journey. I have earned millions of dollars, achieved harmonic health, overcome cancer, travelled and lived around the globe, conducted business among diverse cultures, and enjoyed a lifestyle that few experience. All of these successes have been wonderful; but they are nothing compared to the enjoyment and satisfaction I have with seeing others grow and develop after discovering and integrating these Cycles into their lives.

I need to thank the giants that have gone before me, and urge those students who desire further study, to consider reading works by Napoleon Hill, Michael Lipkin, Zig Zigler, Earl Nighingale, Tony Robbins, Brian Tracy, Jim Rohn, Charles Burke, Earl Prevette, Henry Hamblin, Franklyn Hobbs, Catherine Ponder, Russell Conwell, Orison Marden, Theron Dumont and Maxwell Maltz – to name just a few.

I also want to thank my enduring and uncomplaining editor, Suzanne Peters for her patience and quality work. Lastly, I want to thank my publisher, Rhino Publishing, for their courage, dedication, and incredible help to make this project a reality. I'm honored to be among the great and courageous authors associated with this firm.

I would also like to provide some context for the "spiritual" nature of this work. No matter what your religious beliefs, the Cycles of Prosperity are part of the natural world order and the Universe we exist in. Like the cycle pattern of the seasons, stars and agriculture, ancient societies worshiped Cycles because by following Cycles, they found patterns. Early humans that were able to recognize patterns lived longer, avoided threats that proved harmful, and were able to repeat behavior that brought reward, effectively invoking the benefits of what we now call the cycle of cause and effect. *Spiritual*, *natural*, and *universal* are simply word choices – it's just semantics. Don't get hung up on jargon, be it religious, spiritual, old-age or new-age. Try out the Cycles for yourself and you will soon see a repeating pattern of reward that will consistently give you more and more. The Cycles work.

In discussing the history of these Cycles, as well as to provide evidence that they work and were recognized by some of the major religions of humanity, I sometimes make reference to Christian scripture. I hold that this does not make the Cycles "religious" or "spiritual." If you are a religious or spiritual person, you will find no challenge when I refer to *God*, *Divinity*, or the powers of the *Universe* to refer to the great unknown that holds together the filament of our known world. It is those who do not share these beliefs that I ask to believe in the Cycles for their strength just as you would believe in the laws of nature. The Cycles will apply to you if you make use of the steps herein, regardless of whether you believe in the spiritual element. Use the Cycles, believe in yourself, and you shall gain what you seek.

James Tavian Alexander

INTRODUCTION

We live in a time of high velocity factors that can accelerate your prosperity.

Without a doubt, we live in the best possible age! If there were any time in history to live – this is it. Why? This is a period of abundance. The combination of major critical factors coming together at the same time makes for – "quantum leaps" in medicine, science, applied technology – and in our personal lives as well.

The Shift

In the past, the way to a fortune was through the ownership or control of vast natural resources - oil, gas, minerals, etc. The Carnegies and Rockefellers were examples of such entrepreneurs who used scarcity to ensure their wealth. Today, this has changed – we have billionaires like Ross Perot, Bill Gates, and the Walton Family (of Wal-Mart fame), who have built their fortunes by providing products and services that did not even exist prior to their birth. Some of these products are just 0's and 1's strung together (the binary number system is used internally by virtually all modern computers)!

Even "fixed" physical resources, like oil, can no longer be "valued" based on their scarcity due to realities of the age we live in. As far back as 1920, predictions by the US Geological Survey anticipated the world's supply of useable petroleum was about 60 billion barrels - yet by 1998, 800 billion barrels of oil had been produced, with 850 billion barrels in reserve. The mid-East scares came along in the 1970's, but twenty years later, in 1999, US gasoline prices were at an all-time low (inflation-adjusted).

Our technology has created a condition of abundance that extends the size of the "fixed" resources. By replacing a $300 carburetor with a $25 microchipped fuel injector, Detroit has been able to triple the fuel efficiency of new cars: an average of 13.5 miles per gallon in 1976 extended to 19.8 by 1998, and even higher today. This saving virtually increased the world's available gasoline supply by a third. Additionally, satellites have allowed for new discoveries of oil, as well as new ways to extract oil from areas like the deep oceans and Canada's tar sands. Advances like these have contributed to increasing the supply of a "fixed" resource.

We can see many other examples where technology determines the true base of physical resources. Yet, most of us live not in abundance, but in scarcity. We have a mindset paradigm of shortages, yet, all around us we have abundance.

What is one of the biggest health challenges, worldwide? Is it lack of food or obesity? We have wheat, egg, beef and dairy over-production. If anything, we eat too much. Even in starving African populations, the problem is not any lack of food; it's that logistically it's nearly impossible to deliver foods, even free, to war-torn people in chaotic warlord-controlled regions. Our food production capabilities are vastly better today in a population of 6 billion, than they were when the world's population was only 1 billion.

Consider how, in this world of abundance, technology arrives with answers as soon as it appears scarcity is imminent. For example, the price of copper rose in the 1970's and threatened the expansion of the telecommunications industry. This caused the telecoms to look for different avenues of transmission and by the end of the 1980's 1.5 million miles of fiber-optic cable had been laid in the US. Today, most developing countries skipped the copper phase of landlines and have built advanced digital mobile phone systems. In the "third world" everyone is wirelessly connected!

There is virtually no raw material that a substitute cannot be found for – or created. In a world of abundance the rate of expansion is based on technology, which grows relative to the expansion of information.

But it doesn't stop there. Just as the $25 microchipped carburetor "virtually" increased the supply of gasoline, third generation fiber-optics have been tested by NEC and Alcatel (France) that pushes 10 trillion bits per second down one strand of fiber. That's the equivalent of 150 million simultaneous phone calls made every second. Currently, volume is tripling about every six months and is expected to continue for at least another twenty years. The fiber is already laid - technology is just improving the switches on both ends - the true cost of these improvements is, in effect, nothing.

Former US Treasury Secretary Michael Bluemthal wrote that information has come to be regarded as "the key to modern economic activity – a basic resource as important today as capital, land and labor have been in the past." Truly, the key accelerant for abundance is Information.

By 1980, the amount of information added in the last 100 years equaled the entire combined history of humanity. The amount of new technical information is doubling every two years and is predicted to double every 72 hours by 2010. Even our language is growing to express the new information. There are 5-times as many words in the English language today as during the time of Shakespeare. Each day over 300 books are published and just one week of the *New York Times* contains more information than a person was likely to access in a lifetime in the 18th century. It's likely that 1.5 exabytes (1.5 x 10^{18}) of unique new information will be generated worldwide this year - that's more than in the previous 5,000 years ... And the number of text messages sent and received every day exceeds the population of the planet!

Do you see why you are living in the best of possible times to tap into abundance and the Cycles of Prosperity? Are you ready to turn your back on scarcity thinking? We live in the Information Age and we are in a world of abundance.

Consider the Internet. The net was not built by scarcity-thinking people, but by abundance-believers. Those who are building and adding more and more content to the web do so without much – if any – gain. There are over 2.7 billion searches performed on Google each month – most of the results come from information put there by people without expecting instant financial reward. Information is not the only commodity shared on the net. Music is shared – more people swap music files in America than vote in US presidential elections.

What does this mean? When peer-to-peer file sharing occurs, users give up parts of their computer to the greater good. This is an unpaid, unselfish act. What we are seeing here is a gigantic act of users unknowingly following the Cycle of Reciprocity. There is so much of value available for free on the net. There are innumerable self-help sites, doctors who post symptoms of exotic diseases, grief support groups, very specific knowledge sites, encyclopedias, humor sites, etc. Even the inventor of the Web, Sir Timothy John "Tim" Berners-Lee, gave it away for free.

In the first seven years since the web was established, there were over 3 billion web pages created. That is about 1.5 million pages uploaded each day, or one for every two people - and it's growing exponentially. This is a feat that would impress the builders of the Pyramids. There is no government on earth that could pay to have this done.

Consider the way wireless Internet has allowed people to bring sites to life as they sit outside on the grass or inside a café – working, communicating, and speeding up the process of "response" – be it personal or business. Americans today send 600 billion emails per year.

This is why I say we live today in a true world of abundance thriving on the Cycles of Prosperity. Sadly though, many people still live within the old paradigm of scarcity. For you to enter the Realm of Wealth, you must leave the old paradigm, and embrace the reality of abundance.

There are now many ways to earn your wealth. This book is not going to tell you a specific method to use; however, it's clear to me - if you don't have an idea, look to the Internet! It has been said that information is the currency of the 21st century - we live in the Information Age, in a knowledge-based economy.

Peter Drucker, one of the world's foremost business philosophers, made famous the term "knowledge worker" and predicted the knowledge economy - it challenged Karl Marx's world-view of the political economy and demonstrated why Communism could not flourish in an information-based economy.

According to Drucker's writing in *Forbes Magazine*, "webucation" is the next major business sector: a $100 **BILLION** dollar mega-trend. We are literally on the cutting edge of this exciting new growth industry. It's wide open - it's like the Wild West - just waiting for you to claim your stake.

Each day I work with people helping to them to earn in excess of $1,000 per day, in just one little corner of the Information Age. And each day, in my professional life, mentoring such people, I tell them to embrace the Cycles - their effectiveness will increase exponentially.

Whether you are fortunate to work in some sector of our knowledge-based world, or you're still struggling in a dinosaur system, the Cycles will help you. But to embrace all that they hold, and to achieve an untold prosperity, find a way to tap the net. Keep in touch with me, and let me know your results.

CHAPTER 1

CYCLE OF RECIPROCITY: YOU GET AFTER YOU GIVE

How the Ancients discovered the Cycle

Prosperity is much more than just an abundance of money. To be prosperous has always come with a measure of obligation and the concept of giving to God or to the Universe is a cycle which has prevailed in every culture and nation. Tithing, or giving to the gods or to God, was one of the first Cycles of Prosperity discovered by ancient societies and it can still impact every aspect of our lives – including our finances.

We know the practice of giving to the gods has been conducted since recorded time; even the most primitive societies practiced this through sacrifices to gods and similar references can be found in the Old Testament. The act of giving was for more than just to bring general "good fortune"; giving occurred in conjunction with prayers (i.e. goal requests).

Today, we have a more complete understanding of the cycles of the universe, or "divine cycles," and why these work. You will not need to sacrifice your finest lamb, but if you learn to practice tithing and *reverse* tithing, it will assist you in reaching your goals.

In today's world, this ancient cycle demonstrates that prosperity has a spiritual basis: God or the Universe is the source of all matter, and thus your supplier. At the moment of your death, all your possessions are no longer yours; you will leave this earth and "your" possessions will remain behind. We only make use of material goods during our physical existence - the "matter" belongs to God or the Universe, and the Cycle of Reciprocity is based solely on this fact. To keep in touch with this rich and infinite source you need to understand and follow the principles of this chapter.

Tithing

Giving, when carried out in a certain manner, is the most direct way toward receiving that which you desire. In the Old Testament, Jacob made a *tithe covenant* with God in which he asked for prosperity, guidance and peace of mind. In turn he promised: "Of all that thou shalt give me, I will surely give the tenth unto thee." You can effectively meet your desired ends through consistent sharing of your tithes, or tenths, with God's work and in places where you feel spiritual direction and inspiration. Essentially, sharing is the beginning of financial increase and opens the way to receiving.

As an example, "get rich quick" schemes are bound for failure simply because they are based on receiving without giving. They break this universal cycle. Additionally, "gifting programs" are a perfect example of this: they are *greed*, not giving. Don't be confused by the name, "gifting programs" are just pyramid-based money systems that are immoral, illegal, and counter to the cycles. These programs ask you to give an amount away and to then seek strangers to give equal amounts to you. To learn more, search on Google for "'gifting program' + scam". It is imperative that you understand the difference and not fall for any of these false money programs.

If you are looking at a method to earn income or a way to donate, search your heart, if you know it is "wrong," do not proceed. Understand that businesses promising abundance without work, and a charity that promises a direct return for giving, are breaking the cycles of the universe.

There are some that may say they know wealthy atheists, and that might be so, but richness also results in an overall well-being: health of body and peace of mind. These atheists may have a relationship with the Universe that allows them to reap the same rewards. The Cycles are universal – belief in a deity is not a prerequisite, only one of the possible catalysts. Still, an atheist must practice tithing, and they can put a tenth of their money to good works; thus the cycle is fulfilled.

By reviewing the New Testament, you'll read that tithing was an essential practice, both Jesus and Paul extolled the importance of tithing. Tithing was a household word in Biblical times. They felt that their tithing practices not only prospered them, but protected them from negative events in life. The force behind transferring one tenth of your earnings back to the ultimate source, God, was done in an effort to express thanks and shield you from negative occurrences. The hope was that by putting God before all financial belongings, you opened yourself to health and prosperity and to the abundance of our universe. You opened yourself to its infinite source of power, affection, intelligence and wisdom.

Let's look at some household names of successful people who attribute their success to tithing.

As William Colgate, of the vast Colgate-Palmolive Corporation, started out in business, he said to God, "I must be faithful to you" and he began tithing. Just look in your bathroom cabinet or under your sink in the kitchen to see if tithing worked for Mr. Colgate!

John D. Rockefeller was also known to be a tither. He said, "I could not have tithed on my first million if I did not tithe on my first salary, $1.50 per week."

For many, Heinz Ketchup is a household name. Founder Henry John Heinz began practicing tithing when he began his business.

The story of James Cash Penny is also amazing... As he started out in business, which was initially going poorly, he had a breakdown. Mr. Penny checked into a sanatorium to rebuild his health. While there, he heard someone playing hymns on the organ. After listening, he bowed down, and said, "Lord, I'm giving my life to you." He was convinced that, even in debt and poverty, he should begin returning tithe to God, and so he did. J.C. Penny department stores have since sprung up all over America. The contents of your closet are a small indication as to the depth in which tithing worked for J.C. Penny.

Whether it is James Kraft of Kraft Cheese or Milton S. Hershey of Hershey Candy, a fundamental decision from the outset was to follow the tithing principle.

If you're wondering about how to calculate a tithe, it's simple: it's 10% of your "take home pay." If you're self-employed, it's 10% of your income *after* expenses.

Tithing is a performance of faith and by making the tithe it begins the process whereby the universe will "pay interest" on the tithe back to the tither. It is impossible to fathom the mystifying force of tithing – just accept it as genuine. As with the cycle of gravity, it's not necessary to understand why it works, simply take a step and have faith you won't float away. The act of tithing is a process of growth by which one evolves into larger giving and thus larger receiving. Once the practice is set in motion, the results will present themselves.

> It's been said that tithers prosper ten times quicker and easier than those who don't.

The practice of systematic giving is powerful; it rewards every facet of your life. Kahlil Gibran wrote in The Prophet: "It is good to give when asked, but it is better to give unasked." The reason for that is that a lack of *systematic giving* leads to a lack of *systematic receiving*. In this cyclical process, everyone loses. Each of us would rather have systematic receiving, not "spurts" of success. This comes from the persistent and consistent practice of giving.

Throughout all of this, it is important to keep in mind some additional areas of caution:

- Confidentiality: Your giving is considered spiritual – between you and the powers that be – therefore it should be kept a secret.
- Openness: It is wise to give with no strings attached.
- Demands: Do not make demands of the recipient – it then becomes a bribe.
- Focus: Do not scatter your tithes on too many things; this will bring ineffectual results for both the giver and receiver.

Also be careful to pray about your giving and to ask God or the Universe where you should give.

By truly practicing and believing in this ancient Cycle you will find that tithe giving is the best investment you can make. As well, you will be grateful to discover that it is also the most soul-satisfying.

Note to atheists: **Don't look for loopholes!** W.C. Fields, the great comedian, actor and writer, spent his last days in a hospital and a visitor caught Fields reading the Bible. When asked "why" after all those years as a non-believer, Fields replied, "I'm checking for loopholes, checking for loopholes." Someone should have told Fields that there are non-spiritual ways of donating to good works that will enact the benefits of the Cycle. If your motives are pure (i.e. to help without direct expectation) you will benefit.

Reverse Tithing

One of the most remarkable principles of prosperity creation is paying *yourself* first. Each day you work, make the first hour yours. For each dollar you earn, put 10% into savings. This means you must live on the 90% that is left. That is the amount you tithe on (to see why you tithe on this amount, read on). Consider that remaining 90% your income for other areas of your life: your bills, investments, etc.

> The Richest Man in Babylon by George S. Clason is another great resource on reverse tithing. Other writers have also recently begun to promote this age-old concept. There is a power attached to it that is undeniable. I strongly recommend you read Clason's book and take the time to understand its principles. As a gradua-

tion gift, it makes an essential tool to anyone embarking on the rest of their lives.

The concept of reverse tithing is simple, yet powerful. It is simply the decision to develop the habit of saving 10% of your income. Paying this amount to yourself in the form of an investment account must become as strong as the need to pay your monthly rent or mortgage.

Money, like water, expands to fill the container in which it is placed. On the other hand, if your container is too small, money will spill out the same as if you tried to pour a gallon of water into a one-quart jug. If you don't have a set monthly income goal you'll usually reach the end of the month and find yourself short. You might think next month will be different, but the cycle will unfailingly repeat itself. This state of affairs is certainly somewhere millions of people dwell as they wallow in poverty consciousness. Thankfully, it doesn't have to be that way once you begin reverse tithing. This is one of the most powerful and effective strategies for creating wealth - *paying yourself first*.

Start looking monthly. When you pay your bills, the first payment you make is to yourself. Decide on an amount you can commit to for at least six months and immediately pay that "bill" by depositing the money into your brokerage, mutual fund, investment, or retirement account. Select something that is paying you compound interest and which is not easy to withdraw funds from. If done right, you'll never take from your capital base. If necessary, you can eventually borrow against it, or use some of the interest, but remember what Einstein said: "The most powerful force in the universe is compound interest."

Remember to pay yourself first even if you believe it is not financially feasible! Pay your other obligations afterwards as usual. If you do not have enough money to cover all the expenses, write down the amount you are short and then use the other techniques we have in this book to find a way to generate the additional resources.

If you think this could be too difficult, answer this question for yourself:

Is the pain of giving up non-essentials - lattés, cable TV, junk food - greater than the pain of being in poverty?

If you are using debt as a means of maintaining your lifestyle, then the problem will only grow worse. Taking control of your finances creates a sense of empowerment that you receive when activating the other cycles found in this book, and like all habits - once started - it becomes easier. The feeling of watching your savings grow is part of the feedback loop that completes this cycle, and that will aid you in reinforcing all the other ways you use the Cycles of Prosperity.

A great way to visualize the positive effects of interest on your savings is to think of a snowball rolling downhill. It starts as a small object, but as it picks up mass and the speed quickens, and very quickly you have a boulder. Of course, the reverse is true as well - keep borrowing to finance your lifestyle, and soon the compounding effect of the interest will cripple you.

Honor Yourself

Once you make a promise, be sure to keep it. We cannot lapse into that horrible habit of lying to ourselves. In order to be prosperous, you must honor your commitment to yourself as well, and equally to others.

Don't allow yourself any slack. Missing one "payment" will lead you to miss another, and another, until you have given up paying yourself altogether. The *activating* part of Reverse Tithing is not the amount of money you are saving, but the persistence with which you are doing it.

> Remember, we cannot love someone else more then we love ourselves, and we cannot be honest with others if we are not honest with ourselves.

The habit of saving money should be developed the same as basic habits like bathing or washing your hands before a meal. By reading George Clason's book as well as <u>Rich Dad, Poor Dad</u> by Robert T. Kiyosaki and <u>The Automatic Millionaire</u> by David Bach, you will reinforce your understanding of vital benefits from the reverse tithing concept.

Some readers have asked me: "What comes first: Tithing or Reverse Tithing?" Paying yourself first is considered an "expense" because it is like a capital investment, you are putting this amount aside to earn interest or as an investment from which you'll eventually draw from for your own use. It is when you withdraw the funds that you will use that amount in your tithe calculation. By doing this, you are eventually tithing more. That is why you "pay yourself first," then tithe on the remaining amount.

Compensation

Now we will consider additional fundamentals of prosperity and look at the roots. Most importantly, we will consider how each of us will reach our own prosperity.

Generally, prosperity is attained through the accumulation of compensation received. When you provide a service or product to someone and receive something in return, this becomes your compensation. Scientists reference this basic truth as action and reaction. Similarly, economists call it the law of supply and demand.

Ralph Waldo Emerson spoke extensively on the subject in his essay, *Compensation*. He described the cycle of compensation as the "Law of Laws." Emerson proposed:

> ... this Law of Laws which the pulpit, the senate, and the college deny, is hourly preached in all markets and workshops ... All things are double, one against another. — Tit for tat; an eye for an eye; a tooth for a tooth; blood for blood; measure for measure; love for love. — Give and it shall be given you. — He that watereth shall be watered himself. — What will you have? quoth God; pay for it and take it ...

Emerson was also clear to explain that "All the old abuses in society...all unjust accumulations of property and power are avenged in the same manner." It is not the accumulation of wealth that is wrong, it is the methods in which some choose to reach their desired level of prosperity that is to blame for *dishonorable* prosperity. Sometimes those who do attempt to achieve wealth in dishonorable ways are glamorized in Hollywood or the press.

It may not always appear that this cycle of compensation works when we see people getting positive results who do not deserve it. When this happens, remember that all is not as it may appear to be. Eventually they may suffer in health, wealth and happiness if they are not supported by the right thoughts and feelings and if they do not act honorably. The world is full of examples of dishonorable men and women who met their just reward.

Kenneth Lay, the former Enron Board Chair and Chief Executive Officer, and Jeffrey Skilling, former Enron Chief Executive Officer and Chief Operating Officer, went on trial for their part in the Enron fraud scandal in January 2006. Lay and Skilling were convicted. On July 5, 2006, Lay died at age 64 while vacationing in Aspen, Colorado, after suffering a heart attack. Skilling was convicted and sentenced to 24 years in prison.

Martha Stewart, now a convicted felon, is another example of compensation. For someone as elitist as Stewart, the public humiliation of being proven a liar was more damaging than the prison sentence.

Ultimately, the cycle of compensation will in some way balance the accounts of those who act without honor. We may never see this because many of them will go to extremes to hide their infamy; however, because of the information passage via the Internet today, many are experiencing the balancing power of the cycle of compensation while the whole world watches. One only need look at the former Enron executives to see this principle applied to those who attempt to create wealth by willful fraud.

> A greedy man may become a millionaire, but he will always be wretched, and mean, and poor, and he will even consider himself outwardly poor so long as there is a man in the world who is richer than himself.

We will never receive "something" for "nothing." We receive full measure for the good we give and pay full measure for the good we receive. This simple equation shows that the power to prosper is within each of us. Our potential for wealth, health and happiness is always present; it's up to us to make use of the cycle of compensation – and we can begin at any time!

CHAPTER 2

CYCLE OF COMMAND

How to Amplify and Accelerate your Desires

In this chapter we will prepare you to bring your desires to fruition by teaching you to apply the Prosperity Cycle of Command. It is with this Cycle that you can release the good that you will learn to create through the usage of further Cycles. In <u>Julius Caesar</u>, Shakespeare wrote, "There is a tide in the affairs of man which, taken at the flood, lead on to fortune." Now is the time for you to learn to harness this force, and reap the rewards.

The key to the Prosperity Cycle of Command is that you have authority and control. These traits must be exuded in all you do. Many people see their existence as one full of enormous challenges towering over their insignificant life. The Cycle of Command changes this: it helps you to reduce the challenge before you to a size which can be conquered. At that point, you will be able to look over the world with a feeling of confidence to begin producing your desired results.

Initially, you will be astonished by how quickly doors open when you begin taking control of your life. Many powerful examples of this are seen in the Bible. In Genesis, we read that Jehovah created the earth by commanding, "Let there be…. And there was." In the scripture of Job, we read that: "Thou shalt decree a thing and it shall be established unto thee and light shall shine upon thy ways."

There are countless biblical examples of the power of confidence and the Cycle of Command within difficult situations. You may also be able to think of examples in your own life where someone exuded such authority that they seemed to effortlessly achieve their goals with the respect and support of those around them. Once you begin to integrate all the Cycles, you will be one of these examples.

As you fully understand and use the Cycle of Command you will find it much easier to solve problems that you may have previously found insurmountable. Soon you will see that the power and strength to define your world and realize your goals are within your own mind and fully within control. You already possess the tools to command your goals to appear, what you now require is the skill to apply these tools effectively. This is sometimes referred to as "posture" - such as your posture or demeanor on the phone when speaking with someone. Do your tonality, pitch and sound display an image of power, or weakness? When you speak, does your sentence lift at the end or rise in pitch, as if asking a question? If the latter, you have not activated the Cycle of Command.

Affirmations and the Cycle of Command

Consider using affirmations to apply this Cycle: they are a common and effective way of forming and communicating your commands. Paul may have been applying the principles of affirmation and the Cycle of Command when he wrote: "Be ye transformed by the renewing of your mind." Speaking the truth to yourself must be the first step – it is imperative that you are convinced of your own strength and authority before you can expect others to accept it.

A helpful practice is to begin each day with an affirmative statement that when repeated will help you to refocus your mind towards the goal you are seeking. As well, you may find that posting affirmative statements on the walls of your home or home office will serve as a constant reminder to remain focused. Affirmations can also be very helpful at your place of work or when you are faced with stressful and unexpected situations. At times when vocalizing your affirmations seems inappropriate, consider writing them out for yourself and reading them over. Whatever your chosen practice might be, being consistent and honest when following the method of daily affirmation and command always leads to a positive result.

When practicing your affirmations, it is also important to work at being as precise as possible. Be definitive with your declarations of command and use firm words whenever possible. Although saying words of definite success might seem like an unusual practice at first, once you begin to realize the results you will no longer question this technique. You will have no doubt that a clear and finite command will be most effective in meeting a specific need.

There are three easy steps you can take to apply the Cycle of Command in your regular routines:
- Write your notes daily for the good that you desire;
- Form mental images of desired results; and
- Boldly affirm and command the desired results to appear.

Let's create an example to demonstrate how to use the Cycle of Command with visualization. We'll use a concrete goal in this example but you can use any goal you desire: material or non-material.

We have already discussed how thoughts lead to feelings, which in turn lead to actions and then ultimately, results. But we just don't "think" of a thought. We must go a step further and visualize the thought as an image. For example, let's say we want to own a black convertible BMW Z4 sports car. We would visualize a black convertible sports car, but not just any sports car. It has to be the specific make and model that we desire. Visit a dealership, get some brochures and pictures of the car, take it for a test drive and memorize the smell of the car. You are creating memories to strengthen your visualization. If you cannot drive the car, look at one. If you cannot find one in your area, use the Internet. Get as much sensory input as you can to keep you visualizations strong.

Next, see this car in your mind and picture yourself in it, driving it, and even with a passenger. If you are able to drive it remember that feeling, the power and acceleration, as well as its "new car" smell. Put feelings and emotions into it. If you continue to do this, you will finally get that car.

This is not a random theory. This was how I came by my first Z3 - back before there were Z4's! And on the back cover of this book you'll see me in my car, a black BMW Z4. I used this process to purchase my first Z model BMW. Back then, many years ago, I had no financial ability or reason to have that car. I already had a good car, also a BMW, but I wanted the Z3. To reach my goal I followed the same plan that I just shared with you and within 60 days I drove that car to my office. Can you see this happening to you?

Visualization is not difficult, nor is it uncommon. Believe it or not, we actually use visualization every day of our lives. When we daydream, we visualize. When we fantasize about something, we visualize. The fundamental tactic of the Cycle of Prosperity is that we don't just visualize for one time, we must practice it daily, maybe even two or three times a day, depending on how seriously we want what we are visualizing. We need to add feeling and emotion to our visualizations.

The only reason we may not have benefited from our visions until now was largely based on the fact that we didn't have knowledge about the power of our visions, or they were just visions without power. This will be made clear to you.

By studying individuals who are continuously encountering challenges or attracting negativity in their lives, you will notice that a common thread they share is their constant pattern of visualizing trouble in their lives, and then dwelling on those visions. They are so accustomed to this practice they're not even aware of they're doing it! For those who have success in their lives, they focus on the positive and continue to visualize and focus on that success, or a goal they have yet to achieve. They only visualize good things coming to them.

Visualization can be utilized in all aspects of life from romance to school and business. You may not have heard of it because most people who use it successfully have not made the connection. They stumbled upon it, and it worked. Because they did not intentionally visualize, and note its success, they often do not repeat the process.

One cornerstone of visualization is that it can be applied to any area of our lives and it works for each application. That is the power and flexibility of visualization.

If you use visualization in your thinking and use your feelings and emotions to center that image with power and feeling, and then apply action to it, you will eventually see the results. Try to focus on an exact image and remember not be vague as to what you want. The clearer and stronger the image, the better able you will be to create a mental picture of what you want. Keep in mind that the brain does not know if an image is real or part of your imagination; to the mind it's all the same, so the more power you can give that image (i.e. with smell, touch, emotion, etc.), the faster you will see results.

Getting that Z4

So how do we perform visualizations? It's not that complicated ... You simply have to perform certain routines and **stick** to them. Here are the six steps you can take to **help you** visualize:

1. **Sit in a** relaxed position. Take a few deep **breaths** until you are completely relaxed.
2. **After being** fully relaxed, clear your mind.
3. **Next, picture** the thing or event you want to **happen.** If you want a car, picture a car in front **of you.** But not just any car. Picture the exact car you want. Visualize every detail of the car from the front to the back - including the inside and how you want it to look - until you have the image locked in your mind.

4. Now, apply emotion to it. See yourself driving down the street, shifting gears as you go. Picture yourself cruising to a beautiful beach with a loved one sitting next to you.
5. Visualize yourself getting out of the car and taking the keys with you. Lock this complete vision in your mind and send it to your heart for emotional processing.
6. Take ownership of that car: see and feel yourself as not only the driver, but as part of the car.

Personally, when I was visualizing the car, I was jogging. I find jogging mindless anyway, so I always used the time to give power and strength to my visualizing – and before I knew it, my jog was over.

If you apply the steps above each and every day, you will find the car of your visualizations appearing to you in some form or fashion ... Happy driving!

Visualization is a powerful tool that can help you achieve the greatness, goals, or whatever it is you seek in your life. Remember to work hard at being thorough, consistent, applying emotion, and taking action steps. You will use visualization to accelerate and activate other Cycles, so begin to master it.

All my life, I have used visualization to achieve whatever goal I was reaching for. These were usually business goals, or goals related to my body image. However, a few years ago I was forced to use all my power and concentration to create a vision of a life without cancer. I was diagnosed with cancer, and as it turned out, I had it for five years before I was diagnosed. I was very healthy and robust due to my beliefs and lifestyle, so it actually kept the effects of the cancer at bay and I had not noticed that I was sick. When I was finally diagnosed, I was told that if I was not treated within two days, I wouldn't make it two months. So, I decided to allow the medical profession to do their work, but at the same time, I used all my creative energy to visualize and command the cancer cells to get smaller and smaller, until they would eventually disappear. I go for check-ups twice a year, and I can tell from the Radiologist's body language that he was not expecting to see me survive as I have. The doctors were just not expecting to me to live, but I did. I am confident that my visualization played a major role in my recovery and in ensuring that the treatments were as effective as possible.

    Do not underestimate the power of visualization to activate all cycles and trust that the Prosperity Cycle of Command will lead you to success and always be confident that you have the power and strength to choose which road to take in life. Take the time to consistently apply these Cycles to affirm your way to success, prosperity and good health. It put me into my dream car, and more importantly, taking command of my health by visualization saved my life.

CHAPTER 3

CYCLE OF ATTRACTION

Like Attracts Like

Attraction is intertwined with prosperity ... You must learn to integrate the Cycle of Attraction into your life. It is one of the most powerful Cycles.

The universal Cycle of Attraction is straightforward: we attract whatever we choose to give our energy or attention to. Whether it is good or bad makes no difference. By focusing on negative things, you will attract more negative events, focusing on the positive will only bring about positive things. Remember the expression: "things happen in threes"? The principle behind this concept is caused when one negative event happens. Once this happens, we'll expect two more negative occurrences and it will become a "self-fulfilling prophecy." Those who believe things happen in threes will keep manifesting more and more problems for themselves until they think their "quota" is filled. However, the moment we stop focusing on a negative and focus in on a positive, we create a "pattern interrupt" - breaking the pattern in order to begin attracting positives.

It doesn't matter who you are, where you live, your background, language, sex, accent or color. Your religion or lack thereof, or your general stature in life is not a factor either. Like the Law of Gravity, the Cycle of Attraction exists and works for everyone once they begin to adopt these principles. You just need to be able to recognize it *and* make use of it to attract what you desire.

Are we the Attractor or the Attracted?

Often, we drift into situations where we allow others to control us or tell us how and what to think, say, or do. Once we harness the power of our own minds we can prevent *others* from harnessing it. Later in the next chapter we will learn how the vacuum Cycle of Prosperity ends their control; it makes room for us to take control. But for now, know that your mind can only listen to one voice.

For most of our lives, we were persuaded to follow a certain goal and it's often not ours'– we either work for our own goals, or for the goals of someone else. How do incompetent or corrupt politicians come to power in a democracy? Largely, we are persuaded that our little voice and vote doesn't count – we thus avoid elections, often resulting in disastrous consequences. We don't allow ourselves to think independently. We live day-by-day and only solve problems as they arise.

It is becoming increasingly more common for people to take more interest in the planning of their two week vacation than they take in the planning of their entire life. We seldom use our creative minds to do the things we truly desire to accomplish. We are persuaded that a "real" life of prosperity and happiness is off-limits to us, and that we must do what is expected of us or pay the consequences. Have you ever wondered why there are so many parts of our world in a state of disharmony? It is because we have been inhibited for so long. If we knew the Cycle of Attraction and applied it in our lives daily, we would have so much power and control that we would not recognize our planet.

When we live by the standards and plans of others who don't have our interest at heart, we just float along from day to day – existing, not living. We are creating that type of world for ourselves, not because we are choosing to, but because we are *not* choosing *not* to. We may end up in a financial prison of debt or worse. We are vibrating at such a low frequency that others who are vibrating at a higher frequency are attracting us. We are attracting a sub-standard lifestyle, a "whatever" approach to life.

If we were to turn that around, and start living the life we wanted - focusing on the good things in life and really applying the Cycle of Attraction in every aspect of our lives - we would be phenomenally enhanced human beings with the ability to change the world. We could literally have *what* we wanted *when* we wanted it. We could then have total control of our own lives.

> Visualize a magnet and what happens when you take a magnet and hold it close to metal: the metal is drawn to that magnet. Consider that power! That magnet literally grabbed and pulled that metal to itself. Imagine what you could do if you were like a magnet. You too have this ability.

Scientists have conducted much research on the brain and found there are neuro-transmitters in the brain that send signals from one cell to another. These are electrical impulses that travel from the brain to the spinal cord, sending messages to the muscles in our body and forcing those muscles to move according to the way we want. We have the ability to attract what we want by just using our mind; we attract because we have such power in our bodies. Therefore, if you learn to use that power, you can accomplish any goal.

This reality is why you are apt to receive scarcity when you dwell on scarcity. If you think about love, you can find or achieve love. (NOTE: if you dwell on how painful it is to be without love, you will find that loneliness increased). If you focus on abundance, you acquire abundance. It happens. This is how the Cycle of Attraction behaves. By the same rules, if you work against this power, or are passive about it, it can only bring you undesired results.

Realize you are a powerful attractor as you use this phenomenon. You will attract more of what you desire, simply by thinking about it, and then acting on it.

Making it Happen

For the Cycle of Attraction to work, it is not enough that you merely *think* of what you want; you must also sense it, feel it, and experience the sensation of it. Put *emotion* into the desire and completely submerge yourself in it. The stronger the emotional desire, the faster you will manifest what it is you desire to attract. Then when you put emotion behind it, take action by executing your desires and the actions you take will go out to the universe, which in turn will give you your desired results. It happens every time, no matter what we desire.

Many people wonder how this is possible. For example, let's say you desire a potential mate, or a good business idea. Some people will tell you that they are all around you, but you reply, "Hey, I don't see any!" This is quiet possible, because you are blind to them, and they are effectively not there to you. However, if you use the Cycle of Attraction, the universe manifests your desire by taking off your blinders and letting you see the object of your desire.

Here is a little experiment you can take to show you what I mean:
- Take a minute, and look around your room for 60 seconds.
- Make a mental note of everything that is green, any shade of green.
- Now take out a pen and paper and jot down all the objects in the room that you remember being **yellow** - but don't look again!
- Yellow? Is that a typo? No, write down anything yellow you saw in the room.

It is very likely that some of you could remember only one or two yellow items, some of you none at all. Even though you looked around the room, your eyes saw all the yellow objects but because you were focused solely on green, the yellow objects that were present did not register in your mind. The universe manifested only the limited items you were looking for.

I'm sure you have seen this when you bought a new car. Before you purchased it, you didn't notice the number of times a car of that model passed you on the highway. Yet as you drove home, you noticed what a big and common club you now belonged to! Blinders can be removed – you were vibrating the make and model of your new car, and your new purchase gave you lots of emotion accenting this vibration. Purchasing a new car is very emotional.

The emotional factor that you place on turning-up the frequency of the Cycle of Attraction proves the old statement "things come from the heart." Of course they do - our heart is the seed of our emotions. When we think of an object in our mind, we then send that image to our heart and we act on it with emotion. This emotion we feel then forces us to take action. This is why, in some ways, we do think from our heart. After we think of what we want from our mind, our heart takes over and sends the message to the universe. The universe will respond, but only if we *truly* desire our goal.

The following formula makes this principle easy to follow:

Thoughts + Feelings + Actions = Results

If we want something in our lives, the first thing we do is think it. After we think about it for a period of time, placing strong images in our mind - remember our car example from the last chapter - we then shift this to our heart, where we proceed with our feelings. Feelings are emotions. We energize our thoughts and bring them to life. When we feel something, we are using our emotions. After we have energized our feeling, we then act on that feeling by taking action. When we take the necessary action, the universe does its part and gives us the results we wanted. Often it does this by taking off some blinders we were wearing and we begin to see a solution, an answer, and a way to our goal.

However, we cannot simply think, feel, and act only one time: we must exist in harmony with it. We must live for the result every second of every day. We must consciously and even subconsciously think about it each day. As we learned earlier: when you think and act on what you want, you will vibrate toward it and your desires will be fulfilled.

The Cycle of Attraction works when you perform three steps. And these steps must be done in the following order for the process to work:
1. Be specific.
    - You must know what it is you desire or else you won't find it.
    - The universe won't know what you are asking for, so you will never receive it.
2. Vibrate to the level of energy corresponding to what you want.
    - Think about what you want, feel it, and act on it.
    - Keep that level of energy strong until you achieve the results you are after.
3. Attract what you want like a magnet.
    - If you focus on what you want but don't allow it to come into your life, it won't. You have to be willing to accept it and acknowledge it. Then when you act, it will occur.
    - Use the Vacuum Cycle of Prosperity (see next chapter) to make room for your goal.

As you become more conversant with the Cycle of Attraction, the faster and stronger it becomes. By practicing it each and every day you will find it becoming not only easier, but also an involuntary habit. You must however, remember to practice it. By making it a daily practice, you will soon see how automatic it can become.

The Cycle of Attraction can be your best habit. If you use it every day, regularly, and practice consistently, you will find that it becomes a habit that you will begin to subconsciously practice, giving you a powerful auto-pilot system for success.

The Cycle of Attraction is working in your life right now but you may not be aware. Whatever you do during the course of a day, whatever thoughts you may have, you are attracting. *It's that simple.*

Ponder this: Do you sometimes run across people in your life who tell you that something happened in their lives, something wonderful they're celebrating? Well, they received it because they attracted the good.

But what about those who say they always seem to have "bad luck"? They always cry: "Why me?" or "What did I do to deserve this?" They have reached this point because they attracted and vibrated it, causing it to happen. The first step to getting what you want is to own it or accept accountability for what you asked for. There are also those who wonder why they ask for one thing, but don't get it. This is because their vibrations or energy are not tuned into what they want, we'll get into harmony later, but for now remember the Cycle of Attraction dictates that you get what you think of. It has no distinction as to what is real or imagined. It doesn't know what is meant to be or not. It doesn't know whether you should have it or you shouldn't. It only responds to what you dwell on and gives it to you. As we discussed before, we need to understand that the average person uses the word "want," meaning "expect." They claim to *want* success, but don't *expect* it. Those who understand the Cycles of Prosperity know that we only get what we expect not what we 'want'.

So, how can you use the Cycle of Attraction? How can you practice it? What steps do you need to take to use it? The steps you need to take are simple once you know them. But you must practice them, believe in them and believe in yourself, or they will not work.

Steps to Accelerate the Cycle of Attraction

Again you must be specific. If you are in doubt, vague, or too general, you won't get anywhere. You must know exactly what it is you want - only then will you be able to focus and concentrate on that thought.

Visualize what you want and vibrate to it. You must form a mental image in your mind in order to see it as if you had it in your possession. You must understand what it is you are seeking and look at it as if you can touch it. When you visualize it, you have to vibrate it. It is not enough to just see the image you must feel it, touch it and allow it become part of you. If it is a mate you want, visualize the mate you are looking for. Picture their hair color. See how tall they are. Notice their facial features. Visualize holding them, hugging them, or even kissing them. Then transfer this image to your heart and use your feelings to convey how you feel about this person. Visualize the person in front of you and see him or her as being there with you. Experience the joy of that person in your presence. Again, refer to our example of the sports car and now allow it to be a part of you. You can allow it by simply agreeing that it is the goal you want. When you do this, you are in fact allowing it to come to you. If you visualize receiving a check for $1000, picture yourself accepting it while saying "yes" and "thank you." Hold it like it's yours. Embrace it. Tell the universe you acknowledge it and expect it. Tell the universe "thank you for giving it to me," and then accept it. By doing this, you are allowing it to enter your life and manifest itself.

Take action to fulfill your request. It is vital that you work in harmony with what you wish and do so without wavering. You must make a concerted effort to always dwell on expecting it and by doing so; you will attract it without any obstacles in your path. Remember, when you allow yourself to think, you will then be able to feel. After you feel, you take action. This action will deliver to you the results you are seeking. It works every time, no exceptions.

Personal Magnetism

Increased personal magnetism is what many people long for. Personal magnetism creates harmony – harmony of mind and body. Harmony, in turn, is the first requirement for success and attracts prosperity.

Problems can turn into solutions when confronted with personal magnetism. Personal magnetism is not constrained by age; both young and old can be an attractive force. You do not have to be physically "beautiful" to use this magnetism – just follow the principles below and your personal magnetism will make others happy and they will seek you out.

Personal magnetism can be developed on three levels:
- Spiritual
- Mental/emotional
- Physical

Spiritual magnetism has prosperity power and can be developed through periods of quietness, reflection, prayer, meditation and inspirational study. It attracts those people who want a greater good and a better world. Jimmy Carter had more spiritual personal magnetism than he had "command like" influence. He was not a great commander, but he is recognized by all Americans, and people around the world, as possessing a quiet, spiritual power. Nelson Mandela in the later part of his life is a further example.

The mental/emotional characteristics of personal magnetism focus on positive attitudes to a range of life experiences and might be defined as *kindness*. Face your life joyously and expect good things to happen. Everyone needs kindness. Some people who appear to not have any problems may have the greatest problems of all. Do not be shy in expressing compliments, nor should you downplay a compliment or an act of kindness when given to you. This would be hurtful to both you and those who were sharing their personal magnetism with you. It's easy to find examples of these people in the entertainment industry: Johnny Carson and Oprah Winfrey have this type of personal magnetism.

Physical magnetism is outwardly manifested as radiance: the healthy "glow" we see in others and can have for ourselves. *Charisma* is just a high level of personal magnetism. This is an age where physical magnetism is often emphasized. One's tone of voice, grooming, cosmetics and hairstyle are very important. But remember too that physical magnetism has no age limit and does not need to be costly. You can think of many people who display this type of magnetism including news anchors and the most admired politicians.

Each of these types of personal magnetism can bring you infinite possibilities. It is about being the best you can be and also helping to bring others to their best. Personal magnetism can be instantly rewarding and incredibly contagious – try it!

Personal Magnetism is an integral part of the Cycle of Attraction; it is one of the most powerful forces in the universe. If worked in harmony with its potential, it can bring you much in the way of achievement and accomplishment. If you work against it, it can only bring you pain and unhappiness, because either way, it works to the same degree.

People who are successful use the Cycle of Attraction, but may not realize that they do.

Have you ever heard the old saying "like attracts like"? This is a Cycle that means you attract or use your "personal magnetism" to get what you are or what you vibrate to. If you therefore vibrate the frequency of goodness, goodness comes to you.

Another way to look at this is by seeing yourself as energy. Everything in the universe is energy. Look under a high-powered microscope and you will see minute atoms in constant motion. Nothing in the universe stands still; atoms are relentlessly in motion. One form of energy attracts another form of energy. If you observe electrons, you will discover that one electron is attracted or repelled by another electron.

Every day you use the Cycle of Attraction. Up to now, you were just not aware of it. If you have used phrases or words like karma, luck, synchronicity, coincidence, fate, serendipity, something just "fell into place" was "meant to be," or happened "out of the blue," to describe an event happening to you, you experienced the Cycle. You attract what you give attention to - good or bad, positive or negative. You now know how this Cycle works, and you can accelerate your prosperity by focusing on attracting the people, prospects and capital to reach your goals.

CHAPTER 4

VACUUM CYCLE OF PROSPERITY

How You could be Preventing Prosperity
in Your Life

You may have heard the old adage "Nature abhors a vacuum"; this applies to many areas of life, but when it comes to prosperity, it's vital to understand. Where a person is sincerely working towards prosperity and thinking correctly and still fails, then he usually must invoke what we call the Vacuum Cycle of Prosperity. This Cycle dictates that you must rid yourself of what you don't want in order to make room for what you do.

This Cycle flows from the reality that it is difficult to know what you want if you exist in a state constantly cluttered by less-desirables. Innovative solutions cannot find their way into a cluttered mind, situation, desk or computer. And if they do happen to find their way, they are often difficult to recognize. Once you have cleared old ideas and other hindrances, it will become much easier to allow new ones to come into place. Before I started using an electronic day planner, I would buy a brand new planner every six months, just to get a clean, fresh start each time. The new planner would inspire me to fill pages with fresh prospects and new potential associates or business ideas.

Take a look now at your work area: if everything there, (except your computer and phone), were boxed away for one year, would you really notice? How much of it would be missed? Look at the space. Does it portray your state of mind? Solutions are likely there or waiting to come to you, but are unable to because your subconscious mind says it's full!

Getting rid of clutter in your mind or environment is an incredibly productive step. Often our lives are so busy, messy and full of the daily grind that we are unable to clearly see solutions to our goals and sometime our goals are even forgotten. The saying "life gets in the way" is a great example of this. Are you bothered by your taxes? Do you "just have to do them"? This is an example of unnecessary clutter in your life. You must clear some room! Don't put off to tomorrow what you can do today.

Taking inventory is part of the overall success formula of the Cycles. Part of taking inventory is finding out what we don't need or want, what is holding us back, or what must be done so it's eliminated. This can be debt in your financial inventory, current grudges in your emotional inventory, or tangible clutter that might be on your desk, in your computer, or around your home. Each of these can hold back our ability to focus on desires and see solutions and opportunities as they appear.

Mental Spring Cleaning

The benefits of this Cycle can be found in various facets of our life: spiritual, mental, and physical. Sometimes, effecting change based on this Cycle can positively impact all three areas simultaneously.

Emotional clutter can be an especially troublesome burden. Consider a relationship with a former friend or colleague against whom you've held a long-standing grudge. These situations can trouble your conscience, cloud judgment and even cause negative health effects. There can be much to gain if you can forgive this person and finally release the grudge. You will truly feel as though a cloud has disappeared from over your head; a weight lifted from your shoulders. In doing this, you will be eliminating another obstacle that may be standing in your way. Who do you hold grudges against, and for how long? The concept of forgiving one's enemies is more advantageous for you than your enemies; it breaks the invisible hold they have over you. By forgiving and forgetting you can release the space they are holding in your day-to-day reality. Move on – you will be lighter, faster, and free.

Releasing these tensions can sometimes be a difficult step. Try taking just half an hour out of your day to reflect on who you've been out of harmony with … And forgive them. If the troubles were largely your doing, then seek forgiveness from others. If you have accused yourself of failure or still feel some guilt for the past, forgive yourself. Once you're released from these troubled states, take a moment to ensure that the release is complete. You want to be sure that there is no need to return, no need to ponder or question any further.

When we refuse to move on or let go, we tend to radiate our bitter and revengeful desires over those whom we hold a grudge. We wonder why we are not admired by some and even disliked by others. Those who internalize secret hatreds and grudges, jealousies, and revengeful feelings, will seriously impair their own reputation. You may think they are secret, but they manifest themselves. People know. However the opposite is also true, those who radiate benevolence, loving, helpful, sympathetic thoughts, and those who feel gracious toward everybody, and who have no animosity, abhorrence, or envy in their hearts, are attractive, helpful and desired.

In addition to removing our own negative thoughts we must be careful not to assume other people's problems. Consider Michael Lipkin's story:

Once upon a time, two monks were on their way back to their monastery when they came to a strongly flowing river which they would have to cross. Both were big, powerful men, so crossing the river did not pose a problem. As they were about to cross, however, they noticed a frail young girl standing about fifty yards downstream from them on the same side of the river. She looked worried because she knew she could not cross the river by herself and night was falling fast.

The first monk looked at the girl and decided that he couldn't help her because of his vow of celibacy which forbade him to even touch a woman. The second monk looked at the young woman and was concerned about her safety. He knew that, if he didn't help her, she would have to spend the night by the river until she could cross it when the levels subsided in the morning. He balanced his vows of celibacy against the wellbeing of a fellow human being. He knew that if he didn't help her and something terrible happened to her, he would never be able to forgive himself.

He called to the young woman, put her on his shoulders and carried her across the river. The mo-

ment he reached the other side, he put her down and bade her farewell. Then he continued on his way. Five hours later, as the moon rose high in the sky, the first monk said to his companion: "You should be ashamed of yourself. You violated your vows of celibacy by carrying that girl across the river." The second monk replied calmly: "Yes, but I let go of her five hours ago. You're still carrying her around."

The moral of this story is not to burden yourself unnecessarily with unimportant issues, whether they are yours or whether they belong to others. Create a vacuum to remove the excess and clear the way for prosperity to enter.

Work to become comfortable with both the concept and practice of forming a vacuum to prepare for optimal development of prosperous thinking. Once you have mastered this technique you will find many scenarios to be much less complicated than you may have anticipated. You will find this to be especially true when facing financial challenges: you will meet them victoriously and be enriched financially, mentally, and spiritually.

With your cleanse completed you will find it much easier to move forward as a free spirit to recognize opportunities, process what will come your way, and determine which options are the best course of action. You can now maximize the potential that comes your way!

Check list for success:
- Always maintain a prosperous attitude.
- Always put your best foot forward – and confidently.

- Dress for Success: Wear the clothes that make you look and feel your best.
- Live as richly as you can on what you have and make the most of every moment (reinforces prosperity consciousness).
- List what you are willing to let go to create a vacuum for prosperity to fill:
  - Habits of TV watching, time-wasting activities, overeating, etc.
  - Grudges
  - Uncomfortable relationships
  - Cluttered personal space
  - Other roadblocks that might be unique to your situation.

A clean up on the outside can create great advantages

For those who think that the outside should not count, (i.e. "it's only what's inside that counts"), and "we should not judge others by appearances," (or ourselves), I offer the following passage on *The Psychology of Good Clothes*, by Napoleon Hill. Hill wrote this in his *Success Laws*, describing appearance and its effect when he was penniless and planning to begin publishing a magazine. You will see many Cycles at work here, from the Vacuum Cycle of Prosperity, to the Cycle of Attraction, to the Cycle of Wealth Mindset (introduced later). Note that this story took place about 1918 so multiply each dollar amount by 10 to understand the significance of the sum in today's economy.

The Psychology of Good Clothes

When the good news came from the theater of war, on November the eleventh, 1918, my worldly pos-

sessions amounted to but little more than they did the day I came into the world.

The war had destroyed my business and made it necessary for me to make a new start!

My wardrobe consisted of three well worn business suits and two uniforms which I no longer needed.

Knowing all too well that the world forms its first and most lasting impressions of a man by the clothes he wears, I lost no time in visiting my tailor.

Happily, my tailor had known me for many years, therefore he did not judge me entirely by the clothes I wore. If he had I would have been "sunk."

With less than a dollar in change in my pocket, I picked out the cloth for three of the most expensive suits I ever owned, and ordered that they be made up for me at once.

The three suits came to $375.00!

I shall never forget the remark made by the tailor as he took my measure. Glancing first at the three bolts of expensive cloth which I had selected, and then at me, he inquired:

"Dollar-a-year man, eh?"

"No," said I, "if I had been fortunate enough to get on the dollar-a-year payroll I might now have enough money to pay for these suits."

The tailor looked at me with surprise. I don't think he got the joke.

One of the suits was a beautiful dark gray; one was a dark blue; the other was a light blue with a pin stripe.

Fortunately, I was in good standing with my tailor, therefore he did not ask when I was going to pay for those expensive suits.

I knew that I could and would pay for them in due time, but could I have convinced him of that? This was the thought which was running through my mind, with hope against hope that the question would not be brought up.

I then visited my haberdasher, from whom I purchased three less expensive suits and a complete supply of the best shirts, collars, ties, hosiery and underwear that he carried.

My bill at the haberdasher's amounted to a little over $300.00.

With an air of prosperity I nonchalantly signed the charge ticket and tossed it back to the salesman, with instructions to deliver my purchase the following morning. The feeling of renewed self-reliance and success had begun to come over me, even before I had attired myself in my newly purchased outfit.

I was out of the war and $675.00 in debt, all in less than twenty-four hours.

The following day the first of the three suits ordered from the haberdasher was delivered. I put it on at once, stuffed a new silk handkerchief in the outside pocket of my coat, shoved the $50.00 I had borrowed on my ring down into my pants pocket, and walked down Michigan Boulevard, in Chicago, feeling as rich as Rockefeller.

Every article of clothing I wore, from my underwear out, was of the very best. That it was not paid for was nobody's business except mine and my tailor's and my haberdasher's.

Every morning I dressed myself in an entirely new outfit, and walked down the same street, at precisely the same hour. That hour "happened" to be the time when a certain wealthy publisher usually walked down the same street, on his way to lunch.

I made it my business to speak to him each day, and occasionally I would stop for a minute's chat with him.

After this daily meeting had been going on for about a week I met this publisher one day, but decided I would see if he would let me get by without speaking.

Watching him from under my eyelashes I looked straight ahead, and started to pass him when he stopped and motioned me over to the edge of the sidewalk, placed his hand on my shoulder, and said: "You look damned prosperous for a man who has just laid aside a uniform. Who makes your clothes?"

"Well," said I, "Wilkie & Sellery made this particular suit."

He then wanted to know what sort of business I was engaged in. That "airy" atmosphere of prosperity which I had been wearing, along with a new and different suit every day, had got the better of his curiosity. (I had hoped that it would.)

Flipping the ashes from my Havana perfecto, I said "Oh, I am preparing the copy for a new magazine that I am going to publish."

"A new magazine, eh?" he queried, "and what are you going to call it?"

"It is to be named Hill's Golden Rule."

"Don't forget," said my publisher friend, "that I am in the business of printing and distributing magazines. Perhaps I can serve you, also."

That was the moment for which I had been waiting. I had that very moment, and almost the very spot of ground on which we stood, in mind when I was purchasing those new suits.

But, is it necessary to remind you, that conversation never would have taken place had this publisher observed me walking down that street from day to day, with a "whipped-dog" look on my face, an unpressed suit on my back and a look of poverty in my eyes.

An appearance of prosperity attracts attention always, with no exceptions whatsoever. Moreover, a look of prosperity attracts "favorable attention," because the one dominating desire in every human heart is to be prosperous.

My publisher friend invited me to his club for lunch. Before the coffee and cigars had been served he had "talked me out of" the contract for printing and distributing my magazine. I had even "consented" to permit him to supply the capital, without any interest charge.

For the benefit of those who are not familiar with the publishing business may I now offer the information that considerable capital is required for launching a new nationally distributed magazine.

Capital, in such large amounts, is often hard to get, even with the best of security. The capital necessary for launching Hill's Golden Rule magazine, which you may have read, was well above $30,000.00, and every cent of it was raised on a "front" created mostly by good clothes. True, there may have been some ability back of those clothes, but many millions of men have ability who never have anything else, and who are never heard of outside of the limited community in which they live. This is a rather sad truth!

To some it may seem an unpardonable extravagance for one who was "broke" to have gone in debt for $675.00 worth of clothes, but the psychology back of that investment more than justified it.

The appearance of prosperity not only made a favorable impression on those to whom I had to look for favors, but of more importance still was the effect that proper attire HAD ON ME.

I not only knew that correct clothes would impress others favorably, but I knew that good clothes would give me an atmosphere of self-reliance, without which I could not hope to regain my lost fortunes.

I got my first training in the psychology of good clothes from my friend Edwin C. Barnes, who is a close business associate of Thomas A. Edison. Barnes afforded considerable amusement for the Edison staff when he rode into West Orange on a freight train (not being able to raise sufficient money for the passenger fare) and announced at the Edison offices that he had come to enter into a partnership with Mr. Edison.

Nearly everyone around the Edison plant laughed at Barnes, except Edison himself. He saw something in the square jaw and determined face of young Barnes which most of the others did not see, despite the fact that the young man looked more like a tramp than he did a future partner of the greatest inventor on earth.

Barnes got his start, sweeping floors in the Edison offices!

That was all he sought – just a chance to get a toe-hold in the Edison organization. From there on he made history that is well worth emulation by other young men who wish to make places for themselves.

Barnes has now retired from active business, even though he is still a comparatively young man, and spends most of his time at his two beautiful homes in Bradentown, Florida, and Damariscotta, Maine. He is a multimillionaire, prosperous and happy.

I first became acquainted with Barnes during the early days of his association with Edison, before he had "arrived."

In those days he had the largest and most expensive collection of clothes I had ever seen or heard of one man owning. His wardrobe consisted of thirty-one suits; one for each day of the month. He never wore the same suit two days in succession.

Moreover, all his suits were of the most expensive type. (Incidentally, his clothes were made by the same tailors who made those three suits for me.)

He wore socks which cost six dollars per pair.

His shirts and other wearing apparel cost in similar proportion. His cravats were specially made, at a cost of from five to seven dollars and a half each.

One day, in a spirit of fun, I asked him to save some of his old suits which he did not need, for me.

He informed me that he hadn't a single suit which he did not need!

He then gave me a lesson on the psychology of good clothes which is well worth remembering. "I do not wear thirty-one suits of clothes," said he, *"entirely for the impression they make on other people; I do it mostly for the impression they have on me."*

Barnes then told me of the day when he presented himself at the Edison plant, for a position. He said he had to walk around the plant a dozen times before he worked up enough courage to announce himself, because he knew that he looked more like a tramp than he did a desirable employee.

Barnes is said to be the most able salesman ever connected with the great inventor of West Orange. His entire fortune was made through his ability as a salesman, but he has often said that he never could have accomplished the results which have made him both wealthy and famous had it not been for his understanding of the psychology of good clothes.

I have met many salesmen in my time. During the past ten years I have personally trained and directed the efforts of more than 3,000 salespeople, both men and women, and I have observed that, without a single exception, the star producers were all people who understood and made good use of the psychology of clothes.

I have seen a few well dressed people who made no outstanding records as salesmen, but I have yet to see the first poorly dressed man who became a star producer in the field of selling.

I have studied the psychology of clothes for so long, and I have watched its effect on people in so many different walks of life, that I am fully convinced there is a close connection between clothes and success.

Creative Plans to Achieve your Goals

Now that you've activated your vacuum, cleared the clutter and tossed out your old clothes it's time to repopulate the space. This time, you'll be better prepared to attract a new set of smart and positive methods of achieving your goals.

The first step is to develop individual plans of action and to bring them to fruition. Build these plans and remember that they're only a foundation – these plans will need to take root, grow, change and develop into better and more effective forms of their original selves. To help you achieve this juncture you must visualize the goal and maintain a mental imagine of your fulfilled plan. Also keep in mind that your plans and actions need to consistently work toward achieving their final form and perfect fulfillment.

Most people choose small goals that are really just "hopes," not goals. If they were playing baseball, their goal is to "get on base" - not to make a home run. When considering your goals, one of the most important things to understand is: *you have the power to achieve any goal*.

Fortune favors the bold, never the timid. It's all about risk. Consider Babe Ruth, known for his great ability to hit home runs. His name is still synonymous with "home run" and yet he also had more strike-outs in his career than any other professional baseball player in history. He took a risk each time, and it paid off.

People without prosperity consciousness will never take risks. They will always settle for less and therefore they will remain powerless. Remember, you do not have to settle for less. Look toward great men such as Thomas Edison – what if he had timid, "realistic" goals? If he did, you might be reading this book under a "bigger and better" kerosene lamp! Setting *realistic* goals is like reaching to the ground to pick up an apple that has fallen from the tree. You share this "achievement" with dogs, cats, worms and rats! Nor is it the benefit of low-hanging fruit that you must strive for; that is an achievement you would share with the millions of "Play it Safe" members of society. You are destined for the fruit at the *top* of the tree. These preferred fruits are filled with vitamins, nourished by the sun and free of pests. They're waiting to be claimed by someone who will make the effort to reach high enough.

It's true that no one is tall enough to simply reach and grasp the fruit on the top of the tree; but - *with a step ladder, anyone can!* At first glance a goal like this seems impossible, but with the right resources - a plan, a purpose, a partner, a tool, a method - all is possible! There is always a way, and by tapping into the power of prosperity, you will find it, and enjoy all the juicy apples of life you desire.

> Make your goals as lofty as you desire, not "realistic" like the next guy. You can attain what you wish for.

Desires to Goals

Your next task will be to commit to your goal in writing. Writing a list can sometimes be the simplest and most direct form of solidifying your plan. Develop a list of your goals and the steps you plan to take in achieving them. Remember that no detail is too simple

– if it is a necessary element for achieving your goals, it's worth writing down. And don't worry; none of this is carved in stone: you can alter a written plan as often as you need to in order to bring it closer to achievement.

Lists can be made any time, any place, and for any purpose. Consider beginning and ending your day by making notes and lists. The notes can be a great reference and your lists may be the beacon that guides you. Never allow yourself to think that it's too trivial; successful people use this method to meet their short-long-term goals. What you choose to do with these notes and lists is completely up to you. Individuals may have different tricks or methods that help them stay true to their written goals. Some may share them with a loved one; others might seal them away or store them on their computer.

One useful technique to help decide on a choice, said to be developed by Ben Franklin, is known as a "Ben Franklin List." It's a simple but powerful method of making a decision based on a list. Simply write your concern on the top of a page and then draw a line down the middle of the page, starting from under the middle of the description of your concern. Then on the right side of the page, list the potential negative outcomes of the activity, and on the left side, list all the potential positive outcomes of the activity. After preparing an exhaustive list, you should be able to see which way to go.

> Lists work! They are the building blocks of plans. Lists from Leonardo DaVinci still survive today ... Great people don't make lists in their head, they fill books with them!

Your plans will also benefit greatly from your *earnest* desire to achieve the defined goals. Remember that strong desire is a key facet of power. There is nothing weak or lukewarm about a true desire; in fact, the right kind of desire will dissolve anything that has stood in the way of its fulfillment.

Look inside yourself to determine your most earnest desire and practice concentrating your desire on one specific goal at a time. Perhaps you say to yourself, "I desire the highest and the best in life – I now draw the highest and best in me." Being honest with your desires can be very healthy.

Writing down your desires can also be incredibly helpful and will make them seem more realistic and achievable. Be honest with yourself when you write them down, even if you do not think your desire to be of the highest order. Desires are human and you should not be ashamed: your Maker expects you to have desires. In fact, they are better harnessed than ignored. Consider the scripture of Saint Matthew: "ask and it shall be given, seek and ye shall find; knock and it shall be opened unto you." There is no fine print, ask and you shall receive!

Taking all of these steps to activate your prosperous thinking will put you on a clear and stable path. In doing this, you will also find it much easier to gain control over your present and future. And although it is important to be aware of your past, try not to dwell on it to any great degree, the past is behind you. Too much focus and energy on past things can hinder your efforts in taking the right steps toward the future. Only take from the past lessons learned that will positively impact changes in the path in front of you.

As you look ahead, be confident and remember not to fear the future as many are apt to do. Fear is the #1 cause of people stopping themselves from committing their dreams to paper. Write down what you wish to change and what you want the future to be. Ask yourself what you honestly and truly want to accomplish. Be specific, definite, and sincere.

All of this writing may seem cumbersome – but it doesn't have to be. Just 15 minutes a day can often be enough to keep your notes and lists current. Goethe wrote: "What you can do or dream you can, begin it. Boldness has genius, power and magic in it." The lesson here is to begin!

More than you may expect will come your way because the Cycles of the universe truly want you to prosper. The methods outlined thus far, and those to come, are designed to get you on a clear path toward your goals.

Prepare the lists that will help you activate the Cycles of Prosperity:

Key Strength List

- List all you key strengths that you bring to the "bargaining table" of the world.

Key Weakness List

- This list will allow you to see what skills you need to learn, or whom to bring into your team to compensate for this weakness.
- This is not a negative exercise, it's a positive one –it's like developing a shopping list of what you will need to reach your goal(s).
- Who are your allies? Who has the knowledge and connections to help you reach your goal?

Strategic alliances are powerful, and with an attitude of prosperity, you will attract these people into your life.

Roadblocks & Obstacles:

- Think of your goal, what is preventing you from achieving it? Consider issues that may be financial, knowledge-based, regulatory, personal (e.g. bad habits), etc.
- Begin to think *around* your roadblocks and obstacles.
  - ➢ Brainstorm with others. As you practice prosperity you will find this list will grow with ease.

Prosperity Tip: invest in a nice hardcover journal to begin your lists.

CHAPTER 5

CYCLE OF IMAGINATION

The Top Sure-Fire Technique to Supercharge Your Prosperity

Now that you have become comfortable and habitual with making notes and lists – your goals – it's now time to invoke the Cycle of Imagination. Your imagination is like your laboratory. It is the place where desire is given form, shape and action. Remember: you can create or do anything in your imagination! It knows no bounds.

> The power this Cycle creates is so effective that you may almost find it to be magical!

Every success and failure in our lives can find its root in your imagination. This is most apparent when you think of some of your past failures – at some point you had visualized this failure, and then you attained it.

The French doctor, Emile Coute, said that the imagination is a much stronger force than willpower and that when the imagination and will are in conflict, the imagination always wins out. This has been proven in hypnosis. Often when a mental picture is first suggested the will does not want to accept that picture. But when the mental picture is repeated sufficiently the imagination has no choice but to accept it and to bring it to pass. If your reasoning power said it cannot be done, then ignored it - be confident that whatever the mind is taught to expect, it will build, produce, and bring forth to you, no matter what the 'reasoning' part of them mind thinks.

Your next step toward consistent success is to start ridding yourself of negativity and self-imposed mental limitations. Start imagining your life as you wish for it to be. Begin by forming mental images in your mind of greater good, since that is what you want to achieve.

For some people, this is a difficult thing to accept. I too was naturally skeptical that imagination was stronger than will-power. However, over the years I have learned that while will-power is commanding, and a great ally and determinant of success, the creative use of imagination is even stronger. As you learn to master your imagination, and you combine will-power and persistence to carry out what you imagine, you will also accomplish great things (persistence will be discussed further in Chapter 7).

Charles Fillmore said: "Imagination gives man the ability to project himself through time and space and rise above all limitations." Similarly, Albert Einstein is often quoted for his statement: "Imagination is more important than knowledge. For knowledge is limited to all we now know and understand, while imagination embraces the entire world, and all there ever will be to know and understand." These great men emphasized that success is created mentally first and the capacity for success is first inspired before being realized. Both men were keenly aware that nothing is impossible for the imagination to accomplish – and they both exhibited this reality in their countless successes. Einstein's theories of physics and mathematics derived purely from his imagination. It was not his will-power or "past visits to the cosmos" that gave him his knowledge, it was his ability to *imagine* a series of possible answers to questions.

Napoleon Bonaparte is another great example of a successful figure in history that used the Cycle of Imagination. Napoleon always kept an enormous map before him with symbolic flags signifying various plans for his armies (months in advance of their actual movement). He obsessively built, rehearsed and enhanced his plans by imagining them long before the battle was fought and won. He made lists of his plans and desires! Napoleon's success lay in the pattern he built through his imagination for refining his goals and maintaining an earnest and driven desire to attain them.

> With the power of your imagination and all other things, remember that your intentions must be honorable. Be truthful, true, forthright ... And use your power to imagine health, wealth and happiness for others as well as yourself.

Activating the Cycle of Imagination

Napoleon Hill taught that there are two forms of imagination: creative and synthetic. Creative imagination outputs are the inspirations, hunches and new ideas that come from your subconscious. Ask yourself questions like, "what if ...?" and "why not?" or "what would happen if ...?" Synthetic imagination consists of the rearranging of existing ideas or plans into fresh new concepts. It doesn't create anything new - it merely rearranges existing material in a new way.

Both creative and synthetic imaginations become stronger with use. Desire is only a thought; it carries no weight until it is transformed into action. Transformation of desire into reality calls for the use of a plan. Plans must be formed in the workshop of imagination, often with synthetic imagination.

This Cycle of Imagination is a powerful Mastermind Force. Like the Cycle of Intuition (Chapter 9), your imagination functions well in silence and isolation. However, creative imagination can also be used on a group level - like when a team agrees to do a project together. Where there is common purpose you have great possibilities of achieving it and solutions are often found faster. It is not necessary for you to be in the same room for group creativity to work: today, the Internet and low-cost long distance calls and conference calls can allow you to cherry-pick a dream team suited to a specific task. Coming together to accomplish one mission, then disbanding to reassemble later with different partners, is part of the Information Age and this time of great abundance.

> Today the Internet can be a tool to amplify your group creativity within the Imagination Cycle.

Each evening before falling asleep, mentally go over your plans and objectives for the next day. Create an expectation for receiving satisfying results that tomorrow will bring. Visualize your appointments or tasks being completed correctly. This practice is incredibly simple, yet its effects are powerful. Try it for one month, and see the results for yourself.

The Imagination Cycle also responds to harmony in your life. When you are feeling low it is always helpful to talk to someone in order to unburden yourself and reopen your mind to your inner power. Creative imagination can also eliminate sad memories. Never underestimate these powers – have confidence– – they want to work for your greater happiness, you just need to welcome them and trust them.

Questions to stimulate your synthetic imagination:
- What if?
- Why not?
- What would happen if?
- If it had to happen, how would it?
- How did others do this?
- How would (name of business person you respect) do this?

CHAPTER 6

CYCLE OF INCREASE

Leveraging the Prosperity Equation

The Prosperity Cycle of Increase is surely one that you will enjoy putting into practice - it's both easy and gratifying.

The principle of the Cycle of Increase lies in manifesting and maintaining a mindset of rich increases towards all things and all people. By projecting positive thoughts of yourself and others being prosperous and successful, it will actually help to make it so. These thoughts of "increase" can actually turn the tide in your favor.

It is normal and healthy for people to seek an increase in their possessions, pleasures and business pursuits, and you can be sure that there is no need to feel any guilt or shame for these projections and desires. Consider Nehemiah of the Old Testament: he used the Cycle of Increase to get the walls of Jerusalem rebuilt in 52 days, after Nehemiah said, "The God of heaven, He will prosper us."

You will quickly notice that by just working to achieve the sensation of "richness" and wealth, you will attract prosperous-minded people whom you may have been unlikely to encounter before. They will become your clients, business contacts, mentors and friends. Speaking bold words of confidence and increase to others can work wonders for you and them.

Speak of their success and match it with a measure of increase for yourself as well.

Use the Cycle of Increase on these acquaintances, and others, to construct a win-win feedback cycle.

The Magic of Praise

The universe reacts to all thoughts, good and bad. As praise is given it triggers the Cycle of Increase. This increase affects our being, everything we touch, and every person with whom we come into contact.

Take a look at how praising impacts children: they glow with approval, and then try even harder to please the next time. Watch the body language of a child being criticized by an adult; it is a lesson in devastation. Adults are the same; they have just learned to hide their body language better. The same principle works in all ways, all the time. Even our physical bodies respond positively to praise: you can see someone stand straighter. Smiles appear as well, and smiling produces endorphins in the brain which reduce physical and emotional pain, and give a greater sense of well-being — and in turn increases energy which causes our cells to respond favorably.

Praise creates a positive feedback cycle. Criticism often creates spoken and unspoken negative energy feedback cycles. Try criticizing a close companion to test this Cycle, better still, try praising them to test it! A negative attitude will surely produce negative results just as a positive attitude will produce positive results. Either way, the Cycle works – but you will find more enjoyment in the results of your *praising* experiment!

Praise does wonders for other people, but it provides even more benefit to us. It will change our entire outlook on life. We see strength and perfection where we once saw fault. If you are known as a person who is radiating joy, courage, and happiness you will be in high demand. People will be drawn to you. Leaders and influencers who follow this Cycle are sought out. These are the key ingredients of what is known as *charisma*. By utilizing this Cycle of Increase, you will see your thoughts turn positive, which creates a default mental state of expansion and positive expression.

> Praise can also be used in anticipation of future considerations, not just for the past. This makes praise an expression of faith of the good things *to come*.

You will find that positive results are created as fast as your words are uttered and that you benefit even more so by sharing the good with others. Always keep in mind that when people belittle and criticize others, they do not realize that through the cycle of action and re-action, they are asking for the same conduct to return to them. The golden rule may be simple but its impact is very real.

There is an ancient tale of two men talking, one from Hell and one from Heaven, related by Michael Lipkin:

The man in Hell complained and cried, "It is indeed a wretched place I live in. I feel an unbearable hunger all the time." The man from Heaven asked "You mean there is no food in Hell?" The man from Hell looked at him with his drawn, emaciated face and replied: "Oh there's food, lots of it. We sit at a banquet table heaped with the most sumptuous food your eyes could behold. But we are made to eat with spoons as long as our arms. No matter how hard we try, it is impossible to get the food into our mouths. That's the most unbearable part of Hell: we are in the midst of a feast, starving.

"In Heaven we too sit at such a banquet," replied the other man. "Tables filled with food, and we also have only spoons to eat with. However, these spoons are twice as long as our arms, and yet, we eat very well."

"Come on, that's impossible" said the man in Hell, "If we cannot feed ourselves with spoons as long as our arms, how can you feed yourselves with spoons as long as two arms?"

"I guess that's the point, dear friend," related the man in Heaven, a smile playing on his lips, "in Heaven, we don't feed ourselves, we feed each other."

While you work to invoke the Cycle of Increase remember to keep it simple, it should not be labored or forced. Be honest with yourself and others and speak about it with clarity and optimism. Act-out the Cycle of Increase and apply it in all you do. As with other Cycles, you may also find it helpful to write notes about it. These notes will help to focus your thoughts and can be a great reference in times of need.

It will not take long for your tide to turn from failure to success once you've begun effectively invoking the Cycle of Increase. The evidence of its work will help to keep you on track and strong against the dangers of discouragement and disappointment. The following points may be of help to you:

- Learn to train your mind never to be disappointed;
- Inject a positive attitude in all you do; and

- Avoid talking about hard times and find the resolve to ask others only to speak with you in a positive manner.

It is important to make sure that you are in a state of excitement when you connect. You can reward people with platitudes, and you can reward them with something more useful: it could be entertainment, comfort, a skill, or a helping hand. The better you can tailor it to them or the situation, the better the Cycle will reward you.

Look for the magic in the other person; look for the best in them. Let them know by your words and body language how much you value them. By using keen listening skills, find out from them what it is they need (deep down), then offer what they need that will have true value to them.

> You can increase the power behind the Cycle of Increase by using the same type of language or words being used by others. Their language and word pattern is wired into their brain already, you can key-in on this by using words they already associate with. This concept was re-named "mirroring" in the 1980's and it's a very simple concept which does not require a great deal of time in training to master, simply watch, match and reinforce.

Increasing the Power of the Cycle of Increase

To accelerate the benefits of the Cycle of Increase, work toward focusing on what other people are looking for. Zig Zigler said, "If you help others get what they want, you'll get what you want as well." Zigler knew the power of the Cycle of Increase and Prosperity, and the fact that the universe is abundant.

Applying these points consistently may seem difficult at times but you will learn that anything positive said to others is worth the time and effort. Rather than getting upset when others talk of hard times, you will have the skills and desire to coach them and encourage them to think that good times are just around the corner. You too will believe that something much better is on its way and you will believe this because you will have begun to see the realities that come from practicing the Cycle of Increase. We know it's true because we know of the abundance of the universe.

With the "always connected" way of life, communication norms are quickly changing. Email, text and voicemail messages are often how many of us are able to communicate with each other. Because of this, develop the habit of using the Cycle of Increase. You will be remembered as the person who said something nice, something positive, and something helpful. While we are "always connected," we rarely *connect*, so it is imperative that you connect whenever you can: go the extra mile, and watch what the Cycle of Increase returns back to you. You'll leverage yourself every time.

Throughout all of this, it is also critical that you remain strong and consistent when applying the Cycle of Increase. Do all that you can in a successful way every day and free yourself from any insignificant thoughts: these will only prove to slow you down.

Finally, stop holding grudges – even to those that have treated you unjustly. If there are or have been people that have managed to hold you back for a while, remember that success has many avenues to get to you. "If one door closes a bigger and better one will open." Consider that past failures may actually be success trying to be born in a bigger way - these failures have simply been installments or investments toward future victory.

Apply these principles and be fast but not rushed; it takes courage, patience, and a conscious will to work this Cycle. When you commit to practicing this Cycle, you will soon find the Cycle of Increase will leverage you to a new frontier. You may see the results in days – or possibly even weeks or months, but it will invariably pay off – lasting many years to come. *That's why you need to start today.*

CHAPTER 7

CYCLE OF CONCENTRATION

Developing a Single-Mindedness
to Abundance

Prosperous-minded people are self-supporting and financially independent. Once you achieve the ability to activate the power of prosperous thinking, you will find financial independence close behind.

Financial independence means different things to different people. Some feel financial independence when they have a well-paying dependable job and the security to meet their financial obligations. Another might feel that financial independence only comes when millionaire status is achieved - others may see it as multi-millionaire status, or even more.

You will find that as you progress toward financial independence, your terms and definitions will change and it is important that you not accept things as they were. It is impossible to achieve more if you are happy with your current level of prosperity. In order to expand, we need room to attract more – you need to increase your capacity for wealth. A healthy and constructive dissatisfaction with the present is the first step toward attaining your desired level of financial independence.

The concept of the Cycle of Concentration is to learn to discipline yourself and conserve your energy for association with other prosperous-minded people.

Do not spend your energy in situations that will not bring you closer to you goal. Applying this Cycle will allow you to experience a more balanced way of life.

How to establish the Cycle of Concentration

Common things that waste time include television, negative associations and social interactions, as well as sporting events that are habitual rather than enjoyable. Ask yourself throughout the day: "Is what I'm doing now helping me to reach my goal, or is it in fact preventing it?" It's important to end the costly habit of lying to ourselves. You must discipline yourself with your time and energy. Always be judgmental with what you are doing. Is it helping you to reach your goal? If it's not, and you consider it to be recreational, is it adding or subtracting from your personal goals? Is it in harmony or discord with what you want to become?

Some people misunderstand this area of prosperity because they equate prosperity and goal achievement to money only, often at the expense of their family or health. Remember, our goals also embrace our family, our health, our community and religious beliefs. You can include time with family – be it quality time, time for recreation, or time aimed at your health goals, etc. Be harmonious with all the Cycles and all areas of your life if you wish to find true and lasting success.

Thought, energy and emotional drive are all absolutely necessary for financial independence. You will need a transition period with a "one-track mind" where you think only of success and weed out all counterproductive actions. This might prove to be a challenging step, but a necessary one to help you succeed. Being a strong, confident, focused person will create a side benefit as well: you will attract successful friends that are able to help you achieve your goal.

If you are in a business like I am, you need to attract new business associates who, like you, are committed to success. There is a multiplier effect that will bring wealth to all of you: as you apply these principles and generate wealth, more will come. Spending less time on dubious recreational activities, and spending more time with new positive likeminded people, will cause the multiplier effect in the Cycle to create a powerful feedback cycle of success.

As you do this, you will notice that you have a new set of friends and acquaintances that will be more prosperous and more helpful in bringing you to your goals. These like-minded individuals will become increasingly more important to you. A person's income is usually within 10% of their closet friends' incomes. The lesson here is to find wealthy friends. If you ask the wealthy what their best asset is, they'll often tell you it's the contacts they have made. You will attract these people as they notice your new posture. Often they will see your potential faster than your existing friends or family. Successful people know success when they see it. Become the person who is "going places."

You'll soon begin to notice a pattern: as someone's life flourishes, so will their business. Begin to think of your emotions as the richest gold mine you will ever own. Most successful people think big and dare to be different; they are willing to risk much in order to win much.

> Assume your financial independence now and forget about any temptation to compromise or turn back.

Don't leave unfulfilled goals hidden in the back of your mind – dedicate some time to take them out and work on them. Give them the time and concentration they deserve. It says in the Bible: "All things are possible to him that believeth." Have faith in this truth and consider taking God or the Universe along with your new beliefs into partnership in any new business venture or financial deal. God and the Cycles of the Universe show ways that humans by themselves cannot always see.

Begin to put a concentrated effort into consistently putting *prosperous thinking* ahead of *reactive thinking*. Each morning as you start your new day, write out these words: "I expect abundant wealth today and every day and in every way in my life and my business. I specifically expect the ability to give compensation for this abundance, and I give thanks for this wealth today." Mentally visualize the type of financial independence that you would like to have and start completing each minor detail and then progress to each major step to make your vision come true.

> Visualize the contents of your wallet and your bank balance multiplied by ten. Then give thanks that you are on the road to reaching that.

There are eleven steps to follow to reach financial independence:

1. Meditate and realize there is no reason not to be financially independent.

2. Visualize what you expect to achieve financially.
   a. Make a specific mental picture of what kind of lifestyle you expect.
   b. Specify your goals as it relates to tangibles: clothes, house, friends, etc.
3. Keep your plans to yourself.
   a. Do not tell others as they may become negative, jealous, and impediments to your goals.
   b. Write them down for *yourself*.
4. Take a step towards your goal – no matter how big or small. Set a time limit to achieve certain things in six months, some in a year or two.
5. Avoid becoming apprehensive, excited or emotionally upset if things do not go immediately as desired, nor take set-backs personally.
6. Hurried or forced states of mind produce unwanted results and are seldom satisfactory.
7. Don't worry what other people think. Do what is necessary to get your results.
8. Remind yourself that you are working with an abundant and rich universe and that you cannot fail.
9. Your dreams have already taken hold in your mind. It is up to you to work on the rest.
10. Just as others before you have achieved financial independence you can too. Your success or failure is in your hands.

11. Every mental demand of man has been met – make your demands now. You will succeed if you stick to it.

Some people continuously sabotage their success wondering if there is enough to go around for everyone. This is called scarcity thinking: it's the opposite of abundance thinking. If your belief is that the universe has only a limited supply, and that you live in a limited reality, your chances of success are doomed. If you feel that in order for you to win, someone else must lose, or that life is a zero-sum game, you are living under a major fallacy. Re-reading the introduction will set you straight.

There is more than enough abundance in the universe. It is endless. The universe has abundance for each of us if we choose to claim it. The universe is energy, energy is everlasting, and what we desire comes from energy. The universe will never run out of anything we want, need or desire. It will always supply us with what we want, when we want it. We just have to learn to ask.

It may not happen overnight but it will happen. Have faith and discipline to keep seeking and asking – be strong and persevere. You deserve abundant and everlasting happiness but it will not be handed to you. You will overcome serious obstacles just as many wealthy people have done before you. In doing so, you will have grown and become more: expanding your capacity for abundance and wealth.

The road to wealth creation is person growth.

Many things can be accomplished by mentally taking the first step. Philosopher James Allen said:

"Through his thoughts, a man holds the key to every situation and contains within himself that transforming and regenerative agency by which he may make himself what he wills." The mind is the connecting link between the formed and unformed. When riding a bike or driving a car, it is true that you will unconsciously veer in the direction of your gaze. Similarly, setting the mind's eye on your goal will help to keep you on the preferred track.

It is up to you to choose your path and radiate what you really wish to experience in life. People end in failure far too often - even though they may have worked hard to achieve a goal. They failed because they neglected to radiate the mental equivalent of their goal. It's a sad truth that there's nothing praiseworthy about failure if the person who fails then quits *and* neglects to learn from their mistakes. Further, failure is not random: if someone has failed, there was a miscalculation in the plans or a deficiency in their efforts which kept them from success. It is a learning experience.

There are times when you will hear complaints, such as: "everything happens to me – I just can't win," and "life is tough and unfair," or "others get all the breaks." These attitudes typically lead to a more negative situation and create a spiral of further failures, such as unhappiness at work, complaints about co-workers, employers, the government, crimes, disease and general hard times. An age-old maxim says: "We are where we are because we are what we are, and we are what we are because of our habitual thinking." Essentially, if you are convinced you will always lose – losing will be the only thing you will succeed at.

Henry Ford said, "if you think you can, or think you can't, you're right." He knew, and applied, the truths of the Cycles of Prosperity.

Freedom is also vital to success. You cannot do great work if your mind is restricted by worry, apprehension, trepidation, or indecision. You are no more able to accomplish your goals in those conditions than to do your best physical work if your body is unhealthy. Uncertainty and doubt are strong detractors of the focus which is necessary to become successful. Absolute freedom is crucial for the best brain work.

It has been said that *belief* can double one's power and multiply one's capacity, and it's also been said that without belief we can achieve nothing. How quickly the strong are stripped of their power the instant they lose confidence in themselves or their ability! As Virgil said over 2000 years ago, "fortune favors the bold." The great Julius Caesar took this as one of his personal mottos, and lived by it.

These lessons bring us confidence! Start thinking that nothing can stand between you and what you desire, and radiate this sentiment with your thoughts and actions. In all that you undertake be confident in your goal and your abilities, but remember too that radiating good thoughts is not enough. There are effective steps that will also need to be taken. Think of the positive thoughts as your foundation and a source of strength for the road ahead. Further steps will be revealed to you in the upcoming chapters.

Persistence

The power of persistence is shown when Jesus said, "No man, having put his hand to the plough and looking back, is fit for the kingdom of God." Prosperity is your divine, universal, birthright. Claim it and don't look back; you cannot persist with half measures.

When you show persistence it is often called the "can-do" attitude. Many great people had this attitude, including Thomas Edison and Colonel Sanders.

In 1876, in Menlo Park, New Jersey, Edison founded his famous "Invention Factory." While "The Wizard of Menlo Park" was a demanding employer and a workaholic, he did not resent failures in the lab, instead, he would say, "That's one more way it won't work, so we're closer to a solution." He did not give up and he would go far to employ such a persistent "can-do" attitude.

We know that when Thomas Edison was seeking to invent the electric light bulb he didn't make it on the first try. Nor did he give up and say, "I'm nothing but a failure!" Did he throw his tools across the lab, and claim, "This is just too hard! I give up"? Did he grab a bottle and become an alcoholic and live in his memories? No. When his first idea for illumination didn't work, Edison made a note of exactly what he'd done and what components he had used. Then he made an adjustment to the experiment and attempted once more. And when that "failed" he made a note of it, re-adjusted and tried again. He kept learning from every experiment. He learned all the ways that it wouldn't work. He discovered all the chemicals and elements that did not provide him with his solution. And each time he found a way that wouldn't work - he knew he was closer to finding a way that would.

It took Edison approximately 10,000 experiments to invent the perfect set-up for the electric light bulb.

Nobody had done it before. He couldn't buy a book about it. There was no "Idiots Guide to Inventing Light Bulbs" for sale on Amazon.com. He simply had to continue, failing and learning, learning and failing, until he and his team worked out the right way to do it. As Edison so clearly put it, "Genius is 1% inspiration and 99% perspiration."

Colonel Sanders was born "Harland Sanders" but is better known worldwide as the Southern gentleman with the white suit and black string tie on the side of the Kentucky Fried Chicken barrel. His remarkable life teaches the lesson that failure does not mean the end; it is just a beginning to success. Sanders had many different jobs over his lifetime: he was a railroad fireman, studied law by correspondence, practiced law in Justice of the Peace courts, sold insurance, worked as a steamboat operator, sold tires, and was a service station operator. These different jobs demonstrate that the persistent attitude led him to a successful end.

Sanders didn't come up with the concept for the KFC business that made him rich and famous until he was 66 — an age when many are retiring or giving up rather than striving for their goals. Due to a re-located highway bypassing his original restaurant, Saunders lost everything and was forced to start all over with nothing more than a $105 Social Security check. Despite his advancing age and the disappointment of the new highway, the Colonel was more than up to the task.

His plan was not complicated: he would sell his chicken recipe to restaurant owners who would then give him a residual for every piece of chicken they sold—5 cents per chicken. The first restaurateur he presented his offer to said "NO"! So did the second.

So did the third. In fact, the first 1008 sales calls Colonel Sanders made ended in rejection. Still, he did not give up, he continued to prospect owners as he traveled across the US, sleeping in his car to save money. Prospect number 1009 gave him his first "yes." After two years of making daily sales visits he had signed up a total of five restaurants; all on a handshake.

The Colonel pressed on, knowing that he had a great chicken recipe and that someday he would achieve his goal. Of course, we know how the story ends. The idea did eventually catch on and by 1963 the Colonel had 600 restaurants across the US selling his secret recipe of Kentucky Fried Chicken.

In 1964 he was bought-out by future Kentucky state governor John Brown. Even though the sale made him a multi-millionaire, he continued to represent and promote KFC until his death in 1990. The Colonel never gave up.

Many people have failed the first or second attempt, but by continually persisting they achieve the required result. Too often and too quickly we give-in to defeat. To "persist" means to not give up and persevere on the path toward attaining our goal.

> "Success is going from failure to failure without a loss of enthusiasm."
>
> Sir Winston Churchill

When you meet disappointment constructively you will achieve fantastic results. Often what seems like failure is just an overture to accomplishment trying to be born in a different, but bigger and better way. Often if you fail at something small, it is not time to give up, rather, it is often a sign that you should move to bigger and better things. Many successful people speak about "failing their way to success."

> "Let me tell you the secret that has led me to my goal: my strength lies solely in my tenacity."
> Louis Pasteur

Many achievements have been made simply because some rare people did not take "no" for an answer. If you are convinced that your idea is good, you should persist in your convictions. The only person that is beaten is the one that admits it. The timid seldom attain greatness.

Imagine an airline pilot flying from Denver to Paris. The pilot has a flight plan with straight a line as a guide. But most of the time the pilot is off that straight line, and therefore 'off-track'. That airline pilot repeatedly "fails" to fly in a straight line. A pilot is required to make continual readjustments to make up for their errant ways. By doing that the plane arrives at its correct goal of Paris. It's the same system to navigate a ship. You will constantly criss-cross the line you are supposed to follow; you'll hardly ever be able to follow it precisely.

You must actively seek out failure and delight in it, because there is no success without first failure and the knowledge and lessons that it brings. The most awe-inspiring creative ideas are often initiated in the silhouette of the most unfeasible and extreme ideas. Do not be afraid of getting everything wrong. There is no wrong. There is only one more way discovered that hampered you from reaching your goal!

Persistence works both ways. If you persist and believe in success then you will eventually succeed.

However, if you do not believe in it, the improbability of your achieving it is absolute. Shakespeare's Cassius declared, "The fault, Dear Brutus, lies not in our stars, but in ourselves that we are underlings" and hails from Act I Scene II of <u>Julius Caesar</u>.

Failure eventually wears-out by your persistence and will "give-in" to grant you success. Imagine you are a terrible baseball player but are somehow chosen to play for your local team. It's finally your turn at bat: one, two, three, and you have made three strikes. Now, imagine that this game never ends until you have achieved a homerun. Would you eventually hit a "homer"? Of course, if you had forever to keep failing, learning, and gaining strength, eventually you would learn to make a hit, then a better one, and more and more until you hit one out of the park. You could not lose.

> *Nothing in the world can take the place of persistence, not even talent, genius or education. Nothing is more common than unsuccessful men with talent; "unrewarded genius" is almost a proverb and the world is full of educated derelicts. Persistence and determination alone are omnipotent. The slogan "Press On" has solved and always will solve the problems of the human race.*
>
> Calvin Coolidge

Sometimes when you fail, persistence alone is not enough, perhaps it is necessary to go over your plans and revise them – you could have some faults in them that need ironing out. For example, if you persisted in trying to always drive your car in reverse, you might not find success. The fault is not in the persistence, but in your plan. This is part of learning, it's being smart. Look at your end goal, not the ways and means. But above all: do not look back; always look and go forward. It is not necessarily the best educated that are victorious – it is the "plodders" – the ones that do not give up.

When achievement comes don't let it surprise you. Success sometimes comes unexpectedly, out of the blue, after plodding and plodding along quietly, but consistently.

CHAPTER 8

THE WEALTH MINDSET CYCLE

The crucial element in attracting abundance

The principle of the Wealth Mindset Cycle is purely that money reacts to your attitudes about it. If you think favorably about money you will increase it; if you condemn it, then you repel it. In most instances, a person's capacity to earn money would increase if his attitude toward money were positive and friendly. Essentially, having a fundamental respect for money can bring you to prosperity.

You also need to dismiss elements of greed and discover a more pure and natural appreciation for the security that comes with financial achievement. This is also known as your "capacity for wealth." Some people's capacity for wealth is one gallon yet they desire to have ten gallons poured into them. What happens? The excess wealth is wasted as overflow. Your capacity for wealth must be increased to allow you to keep this increase in wealth, to do that you must change the way you relate to money.

I often see this in my business life. I have worked with sales people and free-agents to help them earn considerable incomes. Often, over the years, I've seen intelligent, hard-working men and woman begin to earn $20,000 to $30,000 per month, only to find that within months, they reverted back to $3,000 to $4,000. Once hitting a higher income, they had become more experienced and thus had learned "the ropes", yet their success was diminishing. How could this happen? It was their capacity for wealth. Their Wealth Mindset Cycle was, "I may be earning $30,000 per month, but I'm only a $3,000 per month person." The result was that their subconscious sabotaged their efforts, bringing them back to what they felt was their natural state. The answer here is in their Mindset, not their wealth-building abilities.

Still not convinced? We can see this clearly with other "suddenly wealthy" people: lottery winners. When a person with a poverty consciousness wins a lottery, it's not long before the universe balances itself. Here are some sad examples:

Machinist Ken Proxmire won $1 million in the Michigan state lottery. He went to California and got into the car business with his family. Within five years, he had filed for bankruptcy. "He was just a poor boy who got lucky and wanted to take care of everybody," explained Ken's son, Rick. "It was a hell of a good ride for three or four years, but now he lives more simply. There's no more talk of owning a helicopter or riding in limos. We're just everyday folk. Dad's now back to work as a machinist."

Willie Hurt, also of Michigan, won $3.1 million in 1989. Two years later he was broke and charged with murder. His lawyer explained that he exhausted his winnings on a divorce and cocaine addiction.

Janite Lee of Missouri won $18 million in 1993. Lee was open-handed to a wide range of causes: giving to politics, education and her community. According to available reports, eight years after winning, Lee had filed for bankruptcy with only $700 left in two bank accounts and no cash whatsoever.

William "Bud" Post won $16.2 million in 1988 from the Pennsylvania lottery but now lives on Social Security.

Evelyn Adams won the New Jersey lottery not just once, but twice (1985 and 1986), for total winnings of $5.4 million. Today, the money is all gone and Adams lives in a trailer.

Charles Riddle of Belleville, Michigan, won $1 million in 1975. He then got divorced, faced several lawsuits, and was indicted for selling cocaine.

As you study successful people you will notice they have a welcoming stance towards money. They respect it. However, when you study the less successful, you will find an attitude of "something is wrong with being prosperous." These same people will often discount the importance of money and yet they also admit that they are working very hard to get it. Having the right attitude and appreciation for money will better prepare you for a successful future. When something unexpected happens, those without an understanding of the Wealth Mindset Cycle will repel its financial potential.

Some judgments against financial success are incorrectly rooted in Christianity. Looking again at the most misunderstood and misquoted biblical passage about money (found in a warning to Timothy): "...money is the root to all kinds of evil." On the surface, it may seem that an appreciation of money is wrong. However, if we dig a little deeper you will see that there is more to this statement than you would first expect. The proper verse found in Timothy 6:10 is actually: "The *love* of money is the root of all evil." Note the important difference here, "loving" money, or worshiping it is wrong, it causes people to gamble (purchase lottery tickets, etc). It's not money, nor any amount of it – large or small – that is "evil." Money can purchase health care, shelter and education, it can also help relieve stress, open the world, and provide employment to others. It can do so much *good*!

Consider that Paul also said to Timothy: "Charge them that are rich in this present world, that they be not high-minded, not have their hopes set on the uncertainty of riches, but on God who gives us richly all things to enjoy." The impression given here is that there is nothing wrong with money or wanting money; Paul is correctly saying that riches are a God-given medium of exchange and that money is good when rightly used.

> If you are honorable in earning money and honorable in using money, then there is no reason to feel guilt or shame.

It is also helpful to invoke the golden rule in your practice of prosperous thinking. You must be careful not to think or say things about others that you would not want to happen to you. For example, do not say: "I am prosperous, but Mr. & Mrs. Smith do not have a cent to their name," or "Mr. & Mrs. Ryan do not deserve their wealth." Through such talk you are inviting negative events into your life. In a similar vein, any envy of other's wealth is only going to toil in opposition to you; it is better to rejoice in the prosperity of others and to congratulate them on their success.

Poverty Consciousness versus Prosperity Consciousness

It is clearly against the Cyclonic System for a person to remain in a situation where they will be continually subjected to the soul-destroying and unhealthy pressure of poverty. It is healthy to do everything in your power to take yourself and your loved ones away from such a delimiting environment. The means to do this will be revealed by putting the principles of this book into practice. In short, it is a step to empowerment.

Prosperity begins in the mind but it's impossible to achieve with poverty consciousness. Like weeds in the garden, a poverty mentality is hostile to the growth of prosperity and is also an opportunist, overtaking healthy prosperous decisions. You will not attract affluence with a poverty-stricken attitude. We must assume prosperity in our mind long before it will appear, but appear it will.

Know that it is *not* your place to be poor.

You must be careful to root-out poverty consciousness, even after you "think" you are on your way to riches. I remember when I first decided to become wealthy: I was broke, lived in a rented room, and owned two second-hand suits. I borrowed some funds (OPM – Other People's Money) to get myself into a business, and began creating an income for myself very quickly. Due to a lack of funds, I had been forced to maneuver and circumvent my way around major purchases that could have helped me become more successful faster, but I made do with what I could. Still, slowly, I did succeed.

However, because I had started my business without any money, coming from physical and mental poverty, I treated everyone I met in my business the same way. When I had new associates join me in the endeavor, I'd tell them they could get by without most of the business tools that would have made their incomes grow faster. I had been broke, and was treating them the same way – with a scarcity mentality. Finally, a successful businessman who joined me said he was happy to purchase all these items even though I felt they were unnecessary. He simply stated, "I can afford them, and I can see their value, just because you found a work-a-round, doesn't mean I have to." It was then that I realized I was still hanging-on to being broke, even whilst I was earning over $10K per month, (quite a sum in the 1980s). It was an invaluable lesson to learn: Dumping a scarcity or poverty mentality is more important than just finding a way to earn money. After this lesson, I corrected my mindset, and went on to triple my income very quickly.

Consider one of the differences between the poor and their wealthy counterparts: Poor people will borrow to finance pleasure (e.g. vacations, a stereo, a new High Definition TV system) but they won't borrow money to finance a business. They will be armed with countless excuses: "Borrow money for a business venture? What guarantees do I have? It's too risky. How do I know it will work?" On the other hand, wealthy people will *exclusively* borrow money to finance business or investments. They never use their own funds. Why would they? Have you heard the acronym OPM? It stands for "Other People's Money." The prosperous-minded person will only use funds invested by *others* to finance their own dreams – it makes sense to them. They may not borrow money and pay interest for a vacation or entertainment system that could not provide financial return, however they would happily pay interest on a business loan that is invested in a strategic venture. For these loans, the interest is even tax-deductible and is paid back by the eventual profits or equity from the initial investment. Even the tax system favors the wealth conscious person.

Consider these habits when you next reach for your credit card: is the purchase you are about to make a purchase of wealth or a purchase of poverty? It is imperative to plan your spending and to be conscious of every dollar. Consider speaking with a financial planner to ensure your bank accounts, loans, and savings plans are positioned as efficiently and effectively as possible. Even if you are not in good financial shape at the moment, there are basic steps you can take to improve your situation. You must have a starting point, and you must take a financial inventory – even of your debts. The path to financial freedom is not as far and long as you might think, but it starts with knowledge.

Thoughts determine our life's circumstances and the conditions of our financial situation. Our poverty or wealth, the numbers and types of friends we have, and whether we are in discord or harmony with our environment, are all conditions that are largely outcomes of our thoughts and ideas.

Your achievements and successes will arrive by way of a completely scientific psychological method. Those who achieve prosperity have known that they would become prosperous. You must build faith in your ability to earn money. This process cannot be started with a mind full of doubts or fears – which is the sum of "talking poverty" and "thinking poverty." You will turn your face towards your goal, determined to reach it, and will not admit the possibility of failure.

Remember: the reality is that we get what we *expect*, not just what we *want*. You can see this phenomenon in varying degrees of business or in retail stores. When a sales person calls on a prospect they always *want* to make a sale, but rarely *expect* one; as a result, they get what they expect, not what they want. Until now, you wanted to achieve wealth and property, but you expected mediocrity. In turn, you got what you expected. Soon you will merge the two – you will want and expect the same thing; it is only then that you will get it!

> The next time you're in a shopping center look for a line up – chances are it's to buy a lottery ticket. Ask a ticket buyer if they *want* to win. Then ask them if they *expect* to win. The lottery is essentially a tax levied on those with a poverty consciousness.

Those who *expect* prosperity are constantly creating money in their mind. Opportunities suddenly "come their way"; ideas suddenly stream into their conscious mind, and then their mind begins the task of building prosperity's foundation and structure.

Through positive attitudes toward money that the Wealth Mindset Cycle brings, you can make money work for you, instead of you working for money. To reach this level of thought control you must release any mixed feelings you may have regarding money. From there you will be able to cultivate the habit of appreciating money and learn not to be ashamed of it.

> Do not sneer at money, nor make a god of it.

Once you have mastered this Cycle it will manifest itself in your posture, your walk, your voice and tone.

How you look at expensive items will change, the envy will be gone, and healthy desire will appear. As we discussed before, we are not in competition to earn more than *others*, but to earn more than *we* had before.

Remember as well, that money should not sit idle: it is the dynamic movement of money that brings prosperity to each of us. In order to guide you in this, employ the old saying: "it takes money to make money."

Some other scenarios may come to you for which you may initially feel unprepared. Consider the following:

- Charitable Requests
    - As your money circulates you will also be called upon to make a donation to an individual or cause. When this occurs, do not give it with the thought of need or obligations – give it to add to their prosperity.
    - This attitude makes both the giver and receiver feel richer. It will change your posture, your body language and your self esteem will grow, creating a better image and attracting people to you.
- Thoughts of Poverty
    - Stay clear of the seeds of poverty; they lurk within reach of all of us.
    - Be careful of negative thoughts and saying that you cannot afford something. Consider instead that "it is not wise to undertake certain financial matters at this time."
    - Openly discussing financial challenges will also put you at further risk and could extend or worsen the situation.

> It's easy to fall into this trap; many financial sales organizations are designing their sales talk to generate fear and create a feeling of scarcity. You will hear them saying things like, "if you don't buy a retirement mutual fund you will be in trouble." As a former vice president for a mutual funds company I saw this approach as commonplace. You must not "buy into" this. Instead, focus on your relationship with money, and take control of your own finances so that you are wealthy long before the age of retirement.

- Additional Sources of Wealth
  > When additional wealth comes your way by gift or payment, it is important to always be gracious.

  > Suggesting that it is unnecessary will lend a negative tone to the money and simultaneously insult the source.

  (This applies in almost any situation – except if it were to involve accepting money as a bribe–this is one financial gift that should not be accepted. It comes to you tainted with dishonest intentions.)

One successful method that many people have used to attract prosperity is to form a mental picture of the amount of money that they wish to attract to themselves. Also consider praying about your financial affairs. Ancient Hebrews prayed to God about exactly what they wanted and so should you. Always be honest and open in your prayers and do not limit the potential by asking for "just enough to get by." This is random and unclear–be wary of such wishes for they are difficult to grant and unlikely to be what you had truly wanted. Prayers are part of goal setting and visualizations and work the same way. You must be clear about what it is you want, visualize it, and focus on it. Once you've mastered the way, you will have your prayers answered.

The Age of Abundance

We live in an age like never before. The growth in practical or technical knowledge is doubling faster and faster, creating an environment of prosperity like never before. More fortunes have been made since World War II than in any comparable period. Keep this in mind - your likelihood of becoming a millionaire is better now than in any other time in history.

The Internet allows increasingly more and more people access to knowledge, and it opens new markets to new customers. With the Internet, a one-man site like www.drudgereport.com can become one of the top sites in the world with over 4 billion visits a year. What does this mean? One man can beat huge news organizations. On the web, all are equal. We are on the verge of an unprecedented global economic expansion and worldwide prosperity will indeed be realized by those who seek it. Now is the time for every person to stake their claim as we discussed in the introduction.

Remember the words of Emerson, "Man was born to be rich, or inevitably to grow rich, through the use of his faculties." Be reassured that prosperity is well within your reach and you too can benefit by starting to appreciate money, both its substance and potential. This is the age of prosperity and abundance. It's yours for the taking if you use the Wealth Mindset Cycle.

The world today is full of people who fully believe they are working hard to become prosperous, but they don't find the results they were expecting. In fact, they are so busy earning a living that they are unable to prosper. Perhaps they are thinking about prosperity and success, or submissively working toward it, but they have not truly integrated their approach.

The efforts of many are often frustrated by their failure to be open and honest about their goals and intentions. Some are also regularly exposed to failure-minded people and criticism from others who *seem* to be moving up the ladder of success. In these situations you must remember to apply the Cycles of Increase discussed in Chapter 6. Surround yourself with prosperous-minded individuals and find the resolve to ask others only to speak with you in a positive manner. The power in being surrounded by like-minded success-orientated individuals is astounding.

If this is not an easy task for you, then it is important that you seek opportunities to attend conventions and conferences of your peers. It is here that you will find people growing in the same business or that have the same professional interests as you. Seek those who are successful or not unlike yourself – honorably seeking success. Listen and connect with the speakers at these events. Also attend conferences dedicated to personal development. This is very much like a tonic and can propel you to the next level in your list of goals. I attend two to three such events each year on the subject of wealth creation, self development, personal growth, and cutting edge health and longevity breakthroughs. Each time I grow and enhance my abilities, make new contacts and develop life-long friendships.

CHAPTER 9

THE CYCLE OF INTUITION

Your Mastermind Force for Prosperity

Each of us is born with the power to enact the Cycle of Intuition, it is a Mastermind Force. Those who we consider to be geniuses are just the men and women who had the daring and awareness to maximize the potential of the Cycles of Imagination and Intuition. The products of their actions have been so incredible that the world sees them as spectacular and unrepeatable.

We all have access to these additional powers of mind but for the most part, we rarely put them into use. In fact, although everyone has intuition, most people do not know how to recognize or access this force, let alone how to wield it. Your intuition is actually your "inner" knowing and like any muscle simply needs to be accessed, developed and exercised regularly.

Your intuition is always correct, yet many don't understand and believe in it, and wonder how could a non-logical decision-making process be consistently accurate. Or perhaps we think we have accessed intuition in the past to make a decision, but it turned out to be a wrong decision. The reason for this is simple, we did not use the Cycle of Intuition – the decision was just a "hope" or a guess. How can we know the difference?

The Cycle of Intuition is "clear knowledge" – it's an insight– knowledge gained without factual, rational or logical information. Thinking graphically, it's like a lightning flash. That's intuition. Or imagine a key: intuition is like a key that opens a door to unlock answers.

Jonas Salk, best known for the development of the first polio vaccine, knew a lot about the Cycle of Intuition. He said, "I wonder what my intuition will give me like gifts from the sea." It's the Cycle of Intuitive that tells the rational brain where to seek an answer. These two parts of our mind go back and forth like a cycle, intuitive brain and the rational brain. It doesn't matter which mind starts the cycle but it certainly goes back and forth, as all decision making, and problem solving is an integration of the cycle.

> It is through intuition that musicians, artists and writers create their art. Think of Mozart, Michelangelo, DaVinci, Shakespeare and Bach: individuals who connected with their intuitions and imagination, allowing them to produce some of the world's greatest treasures.

Skepticism is the greatest challenge that hinders people from using their intuition. They're waiting for some proof of its potential and consequently they hesitate to follow its direction. They need to understand that intuition is not about reason; intuition is a sense of mind that doesn't need explanations. Intuitions will appear to you as both inner and outer messages – but you need to first learn to recognize them. Once recognized, you can then open the door to let them in.

Types of Intuition

There are both "yes" and "no" types of intuition. The "yes" type comes silently–if you ignore or miss a "yes" it will not come again until acted upon. A "no" type message from your intuition is more obvious and is much harder to ignore.

In order to develop this ability to call upon the "yes" and "no" powers of your intuition, understand that intuition is like a compass: it simply points and offers no explanation. Also trust that intuition is there to help you; trusting will help you to magnify its message. Becoming comfortable with these two guidelines will help you discover and master this innate ability we've introduced to you.

True accomplishments in this day and age come to people who dare to be different and many successful organizations are beginning to realize that too much conformity leads to stagnation and production decline. Sometimes intuition tells us how to turn a mistake into a triumph.

3M is a company noted for innovation and their Post-it notes are an excellent example of in-house intuition. In the course of trying to produce stronger adhesives, Dr. Spence Silver hit on a formula with weak adhesion but a unique potential for repeat use. He passed the information on and Art Fry's intuition identified a use for it – first as a bookmark, then as a means of communication. This is a great illustration of how intuition can result in a completely new and hugely successful product that people didn't know they needed until it was offered to them.

Another example was Sony co-founder Masaru Ibuka who asked his R&D people to design a lightweight portable playback device so he could listen to music on plane trips. The result was the prototype Walkman. Sony CEO Akio Morita's intuition recognized the true potential of this product. Even though the company was in financial trouble at the time and most of its directors wanted to concentrate on television and video products, Morita's intuition and determination prevailed. The Walkman hit the market a mere four months later and became a global phenomenon.

This does not mean you need to be a maverick or powerful CEO – but listening to your intuition can put you far ahead of the competition.

Say to yourself regularly: "Intuition is now showing me the way. In me and through me, and in and through all connected to me, intuition will produce the perfect direction and outcome quickly and easily, providing the ideal result." You will find that with this knowledge and belief, things come more easily to you. You will not have to try to scheme and manipulate people or events. You will find through your intuition that all things are already within your reach. You will notice your abilities will be increased and you will reach your goals faster than you would have imagined.

You'll need to get used to surprises and to welcoming them, as intuition sometimes reveals itself in outer ways – even through prompting that comes from friends, the media or other sources. Sometimes this is called *serendipitous*.

It is also sensible to simply ask for direct knowledge from those that you feel could help you directly. As well, be careful not to discount those who you don't feel could help you; often you are not aware of whom or what they may know. Although your intuition may be strong, assistance from others can go a long way and sometimes more than one person must contribute on a project before it's complete. If things don't work out exactly as expected at first, don't be discouraged: intuition will eventually lead you to your desired direction or result.

It was through the Cycle of Intuition that Edison found the solution for the incandescent electric light. It was passed to him by his subconscious mind in a dream as he lay asleep. Edison slept only three to four hours a night and took several fifteen-minute power-naps each day to make up for the difference. His challenge was getting a wire to glow as an electric current passed through it, but without the wire burning out. During one power-nap, Mr. Edison had a lucid dream of a wooden log burning brightly and then quickly reducing down to ashes. He then dreamt of the piece of charcoal underneath the ashes continuing to glow for a long time. When he woke up, he realized the message of his intuition: that the charcoal burned brightly for hours because it was choked off from the oxygen. He immediately took a piece of wire, put it inside a bell jar, pumped out the air, hooked it up to an electric current, and the rest is history.

Mastering the Cycles of Imagination and Intuition will aid you in finding direction (with intuition) and solutions (with imagination). Nearly all challenges require one of these two elements to be successful. If you're on a personal quest for an idea to create wealth, combine the power of both. You will very shortly see a method come your way – perhaps as you read this book – or because of it!

BONUS CHAPTER One

THE ESSENTIAL STRENGTHS OF SELF-CONFIDENCE & SELF-ESTEEM

Integrating Self into the Cycles

The 9 Cycles of Prosperity are closely connected to self-confidence and self-esteem. While there are innumerable gurus selling self-confidence courses, you can be assured you don't have to buy any – self-confidence is natural – you are already in possession of it and you always have been. All it needs is to be activated and turned on full!

> Remember, you were created in the image of perfection. For those scientifically-minded, you can be sure you are, at present, nearing the end of the long process of evolutionary natural selection … In other words, you are as perfect as you can be.

Through observing children we are able to recognize the traits that are innate in each of us. They are born with high self-confidence and self-esteem until they experience things that fill them with fears, phobias and inhibitions. Sadly, a brilliant child with poor self-esteem does not live-up to his potential even half as successfully as an average child with healthy self-esteem.

But remember too, there is a major distinction between being egotistical and having a healthy level of self-confidence and self-esteem. A person who has a "big ego" is really someone with low self-esteem and little or no confidence. They attempt to appear the opposite of how they feel by being a bully, a bragger or a know-it-all. Contrary to these people, those with real self-confidence have a humble appreciation of their abilities and convictions.

You must desire to become greater each and every day, greater than you were the day before, but not greater in comparison to others. This competition is a personal one and it is against your previous record, or situation, not against anyone else.

You must have self-confidence to succeed but egotistical people can rob you of your confidence in your path to success. People can often sense the falsely-confident person almost instantly; they are only able to lead those, not unlike themselves, lacking in self-confidence. When people try to discourage you it is the time to hold on to what you believe is right. Stand firm in your convictions when your confidence is being tested.

Why is it that some succeed sooner than others, given the same instruction or education? Looking closely, you will probably notice that the successful ones are more self-confident. You will often see that they radiate poise and assurance. Others trust them, look to them, and want to be around them. The opposite is true of those who lack self-confidence: it's like they are invisible – no one notices when they leave the room.

> "Getting ahead in a difficult profession requires avid faith in yourself. That is why some people with mediocre talent, but with great inner drive,

go much further than people with vastly superior talent."

Sophia Loren

Build "Self-Confidence Thoughts" into your daily routine and repeat them before going to bed. Saying bold statements will often help to distance you from any inferiority complex you may have developed. Further develop your confidence through imagining and also consider asking the universe for guidance - this can be a great confidence builder.

Let's look at the word "esteem." It comes from a Latin word which means "to estimate." Thus, self-esteem is how you estimate yourself.

Self-Esteem Evaluation

Directions: Select "T" if the statement is true for you or "F" if the statement is false for you.

T F I am comfortable discussing my good points, skills, abilities, achievements and successes with others.

T F I assert myself with someone whom I believe is ignoring or violating my rights.

T F I am content with who I am, how I act, and what I do in life.

T F I am not bothered by feelings of insecurity or anxiety when I meet people for the first time.

T F My life is balanced between work, family life, social life, recreation/leisure, and spiritual life.

T F I am bonded with significant others at home, work, school, at play, and in the community.

T F I am able to perform the developmental tasks necessary to ensure my ongoing healthy self-confidence/self-esteem.

T F I am satisfied with my level of achievement at school, work, home, and in the community, working to achieve more in a balanced and harmonious manner.

T F I am a good problem solver. My thinking is not clouded by irrational beliefs or fears.

T F I am willing to experience conflict, if necessary, to protect my rights.

If you selected "F" for three or more of the preceding questions, you probably need to work at increasing your self-esteem. How do we increase our self-confidence and self-esteem? There are a number of methods that we shall cover, use each and watch how quickly change occurs.

Positive Affirmations

Positive self-affirmations are healing, positive self-talk used to counter a negative inner voice. They can free you from dependence on other people's opinions, attitudes, or feelings about you, and will compensate for a negative environment.

When you visualize a new you, you can work toward a more positive attitude and take responsibility for not only your sense of self, but also your own health and emotional stability. You will let go of negative emotional baggage and be able to deal with your wealth creation in an abundant and positive approach.

Positive self-affirmation will help eliminate negative feelings from the past so you can face the present with an unobstructed view. In doing this, you will develop a prosperous personality: willing to grow, change, take risks, and to create a better life for yourself and your family.

Once you take a healthy self-oriented route in your life you will be better able to let go of the people and thoughts that drain your emotional resources – the dream-stealers – who keep you from experiencing abundance. When you recognize that you have a right to be a wealthy and a successful human being, you can begin achieving your full potential.

There are three areas of self-affirmations; integrate these into your new routine.

I am: A statement personal identity

This is a positive affirmation of the real prosperous person that exists within you. You can build a full list of "I am" statements by taking a personal positive inventory of your attributes, strengths, talents, and competencies and adding to the examples here:

I am prosperous	I am energetic
I am competent	I am creative
I am strong	I am enthusiastic
I am intelligent	I am relaxed
I am beautiful	I am joyful
I am a good person	I am trusting
I am caring	I am generous
I am loving	I am courageous
I am smart	I am forgiving
I am creative	I am open
I am talented	I am sharing

I can: A declaration of your potential

This is a positive affirmation of your ability to accomplish goals. It is a statement of your belief in your power to grow, to change, and to help yourself. Examples include:

I can change
I can grow
I can be positive
I can heal
I can handle my children
I can let go of guilt
I can gain self-confidence
I can let go of fear
I can take risks
I can lose weight
I can be a winner
I can stop smoking
I can be strong
I can be a problem solver
I can handle my own problems
I can laugh and have fun
I can be honest with my feelings
I can be assertive
I can let go of being compulsive
I can control my temper
I can succeed

I will: A statement of positive change in your life

This is a positive affirmation of a change you want to achieve. It is a positive statement of what you want to happen – a success prophecy. Examples include:

I will like myself better.
I will gain emotional strength.
I will control my temper.
I will give others responsibility for their lives.
I will grow emotionally stronger.
I will smile more.

I will praise my children.
I will feel good things about myself.
I will sleep easily.
I will feel less guilt.
I will face my fears courageously.
I will take on only what I can handle.
I will take care of me.
I will challenge myself to change.
I will manage my time better.
I will handle my finances wisely.
I will take a risk to grow.
I will like myself better.
I will gain emotional strength.
I will control my temper.
I will give others responsibility for their lives.
I will grow emotionally stronger.
I will smile more.
I will praise my children.
I will feel good things about myself.
I will sleep easily.
I will feel less guilt.
I will face my fears courageously.
I will take on only what I can handle.
I will take care of me.
I will challenge myself to change.
I will manage my time better.
I will handle my finances wisely.
I will take a risk to grow.

The daily use of these "I" statements is another form of self-affirmation designed to counter negative thoughts which rob us of our confidence. Repeating them can result in a positive attitude, optimism, and can motivate you toward prosperity, personal growth and abundance. Read these to yourself: place them in areas where you are likely to read them. Remember your sub-conscious does not know a lie from the truth. It simply acts on what it "hears." It will act faster if there is emotion and feeling behind what it hears. Don't negate affirmations because you feel they are silly, or you are past them. No one is above positive self-talk.

Self-Nurturing

Rebutting your critical inner voice is an important step, but it is not enough. Since our self-esteem is in part due to how others have treated us in the past, the second step to more healthy self-confidence and self-esteem is to begin to treat yourself as a person worthy of abundance and prosperity. It may seem like you are fighting yourself, but that "old you" was an identity that you allowed others to create. Now you are the artist, creating the identity that you desire.

There are several components to successful self-nurturing:
- Practice healthy self-care.
  - Treat yourself as you would a luxury automobile. Get proper rest, eat healthy, exercise regularly, practice good hygiene, etc.
  - A healthy mind is dependent on a healthy body.
  - When your habit of self-care develops it sends a strong message to your sub-conscious. Changes will take place inside, you will "matter" and your confidence will increase. You are demonstrating to yourself

and to the universe that you have great value. Plan pleasurable and relaxing things to do: see a film, take a nap, get a massage, visit or work in a garden, spend time with your children, pet, or someone else's, consider yoga or take a course in something you have wished to do for a long time.

- Try new things to help you indulge yourself. Compensate yourself for accomplishments – big or small! It doesn't matter as long as there's a reward in it for *you*! For myself, I take a reward after daily prospecting sessions, and a 1-week vacation after a flat out 3-month work session. You can make up your own system, just find an arrangement and stick to it! Remind yourself of your strengths and achievements.
  - ➤ Establish a "success" file of awards, certificates and positive letters or citations.
  - ➤ Keep mementos of accomplishments you are proud of near your work area.
  - ➤ Laminate or frame photos of yourself with those you respect and were mentored by.
  - ➤ Focus on anything and everything. No matter how small it may seem, if you succeeded and are proud of it, focus on it and celebrate!

An enormous step you can take is to forgive yourself when you don't accomplish all that you had hoped to. Self-nurturing can be surprisingly difficult if you are a perfectionist. Perfectionists are victims of low self-esteem and must learn to recognize that this is a symptom of a mental challenge – it's *not* a good trait. Learn not to be critical of yourself and to *learn* from mistakes rather than getting upset about them. Reward yourself for moving forward in your plans in the first place. That's a major step toward creating confidence and prosperity!

Praise

A unique method of building your own self-confidence is to praise the merits of *others*. As we learned in the Cycle of Increase, praising others – in a confident manner – denotes your expert status. It also allows your sub-conscious to recognize you as a leader.

Self-confidence is truly contagious. Make sure that you associate with people who also have self-confidence. They will reassure you in your path and help to maintain and enhance your current levels of self-confidence.

As we learn to build our path to prosperity we see that by expecting great results from our efforts, confidence is built. Due to the harmonic nature of the Cycles of Prosperity your belief in your goals and plans will continue to fortify your confidence level.

When you truly believe, you become confident because you are able to see a way to success. Doubt is the reverse: it creates pessimism, blinding you to positive outcomes and solutions. Belief in your ultimate success will eliminate fears so you are better able to manage the uncertainties that may come.

> Imagine being so confident that you make decisions easily and quickly find solutions to challenges! You will move with the posture of a leader, attracting people to your cause.

Belief in yourself – and the confidence it creates – will change your own estimate of yourself, of your ability, your standing, the weight you carry, and the manner in which you carry yourself. Each of these in turn will affect others. Often it's these others that will be part of the solution, and some will eventually be part of your "MasterMind Group." As described by Napoleon Hill, this group is: "a team of like-minded individuals, who come together from different but respected backgrounds to assist each other, brainstorm and offer solutions, which often succeeds due to the different backgrounds and experiences of the participants."

Your self-esteem and the confidence it creates contributes to your vitality, energy level, persistence, and personal magnetism. Self-esteem is about what is on the inside, a belief in yourself and your abilities. Positive esteem focuses on acceptance of self and others alike. It remains constant despite the storm. This fosters cooperation and wholeness.

This confidence is one of the basic foundations of achievement. There is a marvelous power in conviction. Those with great faith in themselves are released from fears - they melt away, and eventually you will never experience fear, or if you do, it lasts only seconds. You will always know you are in the right place, you will know your capacity and capability, and you will cease to worry about the future.

> Improving self esteem is like exercising a muscle; and like all muscles, self esteem either weakens or gets stronger depending on use. It relies on small incremental improvements on a daily basis. You wouldn't run out to the gym and have perfect lifelong muscles after one session. Consistent self esteem improvement is the only way to lasting success and an increase in the quality of your day-to-day life.

BONUS CHAPTER Two

REVOLUTIONIZE YOUR HEALTH WITH THE CYCLES OF PROSPERITY

"The most important thing in life is good health: without it, nothing else much matters."

I have often read this statement, or heard it from wealthy people, and watched the reactions of those around me. Those with a poverty consciousness would laugh, or even say, "I'd love to have your money and take my chances with my health." One only has to realize that without health, there is no enjoyment of the benefits of wealth, family, community or service. Many statistics show us that the wealthy have better health than those who are not wealthy. Some may explain this away with reasons such as access to "better" doctors, healthcare, foods, or a lack of stress, etc. However, these are just the benefits of a prosperity consciousness. Those who truly have a prosperity consciousness realize the bank they withdraw from is within them – the bank is limitless and connected to the universe – and they take care of their accounts!

Once you have grasped and internalized prosperity consciousness, you will come to realize that true health is part of prosperity. A prosperous thinker knows how to free himself of hostilities, resentments, criticism and irritated emotions which can bring on "dis-ease" or what medical professionals call "disease."

The body is a very sensitive instrument: thoughts, emotions and words are expressed through it *and* to it. Remember we are a magnet, and we can attract and pick up the negatives around us if we allow ourselves to. Where there is ill health, there is a situation where the ill person has been subjected to internal discord of mind, body or affairs. Many people who are in poor health because of financial matters find that their health improves when their financial matters improve.

Philosophers of all times have tried to point out that man's health is controlled by his attitudes toward himself and others. Hippocrates wrote, "Men ought to know that from the brain, and from the brain only, arises our sorrow, pain, grief and fear." Similarly, Plato declared: "If the head and the body are to be well, you must begin by curing the soul."

It is often the feeling of defeat that causes ill health. You will notice that forgiveness and happiness can often heal you. The easiest way to healing ourselves is to make peace with those who are out of harmony with us. You will probably find that among your acquaintances there are people that you should forgive. Prayer or meditation can often facilitate a seamless passage to forgiveness of oneself or others. The Lord's Prayer also has healing powers because it is basically a series of strong, powerful affirmative statements, in which one claims the power, substance, guidance and goodness of God. Use it if you wish – it's a good place to start. Later as you master these methods, you can create your own series of affirmations regarding your health, and you can modify them as needed depending on your religious beliefs.

Affirmation is both an ancient art and a modern transformation tool. Mental pictures are important. If you require healing, forming mental pictures in your mind of the results that you want to achieve is one of the most positive steps you can take towards that healing. When manifesting these mental images, it is vital that you are specific. The imagining method has been a successful method for quitting smoking, losing weight, or breaking dependency on drugs and alcohol or fighting cancer. As I described before about my fight to beat cancer in my body, I asked my radiologist to explain the concept behind the radiation. Based on his explanations, I was able to create a very specific visualization that I focused on to leverage the effect of the radiation as it hit the cancer cells threatening my body. The combination of visualizations and medical science worked!

Think of your body like a quality German automobile: if properly maintained, it will provide superb performance and run for one hundred years or more – if neglected or mistreated, it will very soon get out of order, and deteriorate long before it should. The average life expectancy of humans is getting longer and longer each day. Advancements in science have and continue to make even a life to 130 years possible soon, and that's just the start. This is part of the abundance of the universe and the prosperous times we live in. The challenge for us is to keep our bodies in good shape to enjoy a long life. It is not "living" to be in a hospital bed attached to tubes and wires. *Living* is about movement, mobility, and strength.

Our mental image determines what state of health our life will take – whether it shall be a youthful or aging existence. Every one of us has the inherent capacity for prolonging our life and increasing our potential longevity; but we must first understand how to use the same cycles for prosperity for our health. It may be true that our genes have pre-supposed settings of health or life expectancy for us, but they are only that: a set of pre-supposed conditions. I was pre-supposed to die of cancer. However by using a combination of the cycles of mental imaging and medical discoveries – medical advancements are provided by scientists' everyday that use the same Cycles that Edison and Einstein had used – I have prolonged my pre-destination for an early death. This is not a miracle; it is a logical application of the Cycles.

Perfect fitness, vitality, and health are unattainable to one whose mind is convinced that they are declining, that they are going downward physically, that their health is steadily dwindling as they age. You can gain and acquire optimal health, vitality and robustness.

We live in the times of what the ancients would call miraculous. Today, we are in the wake of countless medical marvels that are being brought about by scientists tapping into the Cycles of the Universe. Here is an excerpt from an Associated Press article on the regrowth of fingers:

NEW YORK (AP) - Researchers are trying to find ways to regrow fingers - and someday, even limbs - with tricks that sound like magic spells from a Harry Potter novel. There's the guy who sliced off a fingertip but grew it back, after he treated the wound with an extract of pig bladder.

...consider the situation of Lee Spievack, a hobby-store salesman in Cincinnati, as he regarded his

severed right middle finger one evening in August 2005.

He had been helping a customer with an engine on a model airplane behind the shop. He knew the motor was risky because it required somebody to turn the prop backwards to make it run the right way.

"I pointed to it," Spievack recalled the other day, "and said, 'You need to get rid of this engine, it's too dangerous.' And I put my finger through the prop." He'd misjudged the distance to the spinning plastic prop. It sliced off his fingertip, leaving just a bit of the nail bed. The missing piece, three-eighths of an inch long, was never found.

An emergency room doctor wrapped up the rest of his finger and sent him to a hand surgeon, who recommended a skin graft to cover what was left of his finger. What was gone, it appeared, was gone forever.

If Spievack, now 68, had been a toddler, things might have been different. Up to about age 2, people can consistently regrow fingertips, says Dr. Stephen Badylak, a regeneration expert at the University of Pittsburgh. But that's rare in adults, he said.

Spievack, however, did have a major advantage - a brother, Alan, a former Harvard surgeon who founded a company called ACell Inc., that makes an extract of pig bladder for promoting healing and tissue regeneration. It helps horses re-grow ligaments, for example, and the federal government has given clearance to market it for use in people. Similar formulations have been used in many people to do things like treat ulcers and other wounds and to help make cartilage.

The summer before Lee Spievack's accident, Dr. Alan Spievack had used it on a neighbor who had cut his fingertip off on a tablesaw. The man's fingertip grew back over four to six weeks, Alan Spievack said.

Lee Spievack took his brother's advice to forget about a skin graft and try the pig powder.

Soon a shipment of the stuff arrived and Lee Spievack started applying it every two days. Within four weeks his finger had regained its original length, he says, and in four months "it looked like my normal finger."

Spievack said it's a little hard, as if calloused, and there's a slight scar on the end. The nail continues to grow at twice the speed of his other nails. "All my fingers in this cold weather have cracked except that one," he said.

All in all, he said, "I'm quite impressed."

(Ritter, Malcolm. "Scientists try to regrow fingers with animals." February 20, 2007)

When you combine the results of those involved in medical research with your own use of the Cycles of the Universe, you can see the potential for controlling your health, and reversing major illness or accidents that can occur. This should give you great comfort and excitement about the future.

There are more people today *working* on medical research then there were people *living* 300 years ago. The combined energy and imaginations compel the universe to provide discovery after discovery – the future is exciting! This compounding will continue into a fantastic feedback cycle. As the old saying goes, "don't go anywhere, you ain't seen nothin' yet!"

We must realize that our mental attitude is an energy which is constantly creating results. Whenever we focus the mind we are producing – creating something – be it a positive self image, or a poor one. Just as the person who says "I'm bad with numbers" will always reach for a calculator, so will the person who says "I have a bad heart," always reach for the stair rail. However, the reverse is true as well, for both our mathematical abilities and our health!

You are never "old" unless your interest in life has disappeared – if your spirit becomes aged, or your heart becomes cold and unresponsive, then you might as well look for a nice grave stone. This is called "giving up" and ending the desire for growth. If someone has reached this point and is unwilling to change, they are doomed. However, as long as you continuously connect with life you cannot grow old.

Living the Cyclonic Life

Let me describe one of my closest friends, Willie. He's 82, many decades older then I. But to me he seems ageless; I forget his age. Often when we are seated in some all-night café, having a lively discussion on philosophy, health, religion or business, it may appear to others that we are in a heated argument. They scold me with their eyes for having such an animated debate with an "old man." But Willie isn't old, he's only 82. Let me describe his day:

He rises at noon, has fruit and relaxes. He then has a great homemade breakfast. After that he'll have a long walk. By supper hour he'll have made some business appointments and goes off to them. By 11PM he's done his business for the day – developing real estate in his office: various cafés across the city. Then as I finish my day working from home on the net, I often meet with him in one of our favorite all-night restaurants. I end up leaving him there to go home to bed. He relaxes a while longer, and then jogs from about 3AM to 5AM. In the winter he just walks. By 5AM he turns in.

Does this sound like an 82 year old man? No, Willie plans on making it to 130, or more. Just by keeping himself fit, eating right, fasting, and keeping his connection to the Universe strong. I've known this self-made millionaire since I was a teenager. With only a grade 6 education he has become something of a real estate and health guru – and a great friend. Willie applied all of these Cycles to build his life, and never even knew their names. A law is a law, no matter how you label it.

A person is old, regardless of their physical years, when they are unconnected with the spirit of the times; when they have ceased to be progressive and up-to-date.

When automated tellers first appeared, were you one of those people who was unwilling to "go to a wall" to do their banking? What about now? Look at the Internet, do you know people who tell you they "can't learn computers," as if computers were still giant monoliths from the 1960's? My mother was like that. No matter what I did she would not consider using a computer. A year ago I gave her a laptop. She was happy about how it looked, but still afraid. After some patience on both our parts, she's now emailing our many family members and grandchildren, she's also surfing the net like anyone else.

She's in her 70's and just returned from a trip to the Antarctic. From being unwilling to adapt to becoming a globe-trotting net surfer, people can change. My mother is younger now than she was five years ago. I have noticed more life in her since she became in touch with the world via the Internet and her travel. She plays bridge online with people all over the globe, and messages them as well. This could be a description of a 20 year old, but it's someone who could be considered "old." She does not consider herself old, and that's why she's not. Keep up with the times, become excited to be part of it – life is not passing you by unless you let it.

Let's now look at the four letter word: *work*. Work and health are very related.

"Work" means different things to different people, but one truth is that many people find they are unsatisfied at work, especially while at entry level jobs, positions that require little or no creativity, or positions without any real chance of advancement. It is at this point that they inevitably decide to "give up" and remain at that level, or start looking for a new job or seek a promotion. This is one time when dissatisfaction can be a help because it may prod them to aim higher. Some people are motivated by disgust. Disgust of their present situation, their community, their milieu or even their body image, and this can drive them to make a commitment to change.

> The saddest person is one without a plan, for surely they will end up working toward someone else's success, rather than their own.

Working in the Information Age

You must have a definite goal in mind in order to improve your current situation. To keep you on target it helps to perfect your attitudes toward work and to eliminate thoughts of how others may have prevented your success. Focus instead on what you can do to succeed. For example, are you prepared to further your education? Would you consider seeking courses on the Internet to achieve your aim? Specialized knowledge is the key to success. We are in a knowledge-based economy – we live in the information age – yet many are not ready for the educational step even though it is a practical and effective move. Instead of learning more, some people prefer to spend their time criticizing their supervisor and co-workers. Others brag about having not read a book since high school! Be careful not to fall into such negative habits.

It is our attitude which remains the constant element that can make the difference. A prosperous thinker might think of work as heavenly or inspiring, or as a creative way to generate good. Kahlil Gibran wrote that "work is love made visible." Work doesn't need to have negative connotations. It can be a means to an end, but it is also best when you enjoy the work and truly make the most of it. It has been said that "if you love what you do, you'll never have to work a day in your life," and "work is the highest form of play" – these are incredible truths!

How you choose to feel about your situation is very important and within your control. Man's true work is that which he does best, and from which he gets his deepest satisfaction. If avenues of expression are not found at work then we become unhappy and consider work to be a bother. This has a major but unseen impact on your health. The power to make the most of your work life is entirely within your control. Don't be afraid to harness its potential.

Work diligently to direct your energy and positive thoughts toward your goal. Things cannot change in your environment until they change in your mind. Only *you* have the power to allow your mind to impact the achievement of your goals.

Remember too that there is nothing wrong in becoming discouraged, but the true challenge is to not let discouragement overwhelm you. Despair is usually an emotional indication that the tide is turning. When despair is creeping toward you, keep in mind the fantastic goal that you are aiming for and do not lose sight of it in your mind's eye. With the right attitude you will always find that the real success lies in a straight line before you. Do not deviate from the chosen path.

Also remember that each job you do, no matter how high or low you might classify it, should be done to the best of your ability. You may find that your new opportunity will come to you when you have mastered everything in your old job; this is often the case. James Allen once said, "Your Circumstances may be uncongenial, but they shall not long remain so if you perceive an ideal and strive to reach it. You cannot travel within and still stand without." His words imply that no matter what your circumstances are, you cannot lose sight of your goal or stop working towards it. It will not simply come to you while you wait; you must constantly make efforts to continue the journey to reach your goal.

When apprehension or uncertainties confront you, march on. Affirm and believe in your prosperity, your limitless success for yourself, no matter your current circumstances. Assert: "I am the master of my own fate, I shall reach my goal." Conquer doubt and fear, and you will circumvent failure. Have confidence in this knowledge, it won't let you down. You'll be comforted to know that nothing in life stands still, everything is changing and the coming changes will be better and better. Learn to embrace change, do not be afraid of it.

As you move along the path toward prosperity it is also helpful to saturate yourself in an atmosphere of plenty and in association with successful people:

- Observe the wealthy sections of your city: drive through and attend showings of homes you desire;
- Associate with creative individuals and people with talent;
- Go to operas or concerts;
- Read books about successful people; and
- Test drive the car of your dreams!

Each of these steps will help you to visualize and realize you goals. It will also help if you always make the most out of your present situation and let go of criticism and negativity. These situations will remind you of what you're striving for.

Here are some steps to keep you on track:
- Visualize what you want from life;
- Mentally live your desires;
- Ask divine intelligence for guidance and support;
- Persist and persevere in knowing that agreeable work can and shall be yours;

- Remember that everything has a price; and
- Always continue doing your best.

Whatever you endeavor to do should bring you closer to your goal – even if it's just to create financial capital. At the same time, look on it as a learning experience. Every experience counts: in terms of developing leadership skills, using the Cycle of Increase, gaining knowledge about the industry you are in, or just learning secondary skills – like using a computer or other specialized information that will be useful to you reaching your goal in the future.

We have spoken about wealth for most of this book. When you first picked up this book, you may have thought that there was no connection between your mental thoughts and money or wealth. We now know there is a direct connection. These Cycles that hold the Universe together affect our wealth, and are equally effective upon our health. In fact, the ancients used these Cycles far more often for health then they did wealth. Think of the placebo effect to realize that you already know that they work. It is not our intention here to change the subject of this book, but to inform you that with what you now know, you can achieve the state of health you desire.

BONUS CHAPTER Three

HOW TO MAINTAIN YOUR MENTAL EFFICIENCY

The minds of many people have become cluttered and ineffective because they did not break the habit of nightly visualizing and focusing on their troubles and problems, which always seemed so much more inflated and appeared much worse at night. Instead, before falling into slumber, we should fill the mind with vivid, heartening, and inspirational thoughts. We should never go to sleep until we have restored our missing mental harmony, or until we have put into operation the forces which would tend to harmonize and bring tranquility and calm back into our lives. This includes a mental image of being in perfect health, and in the body shape you desire, successfully completing the tasks you have for yourself the next day. Eventually, this practice will lead your subconscious to begin making better choices in food, drink, and exercise.

Those who age rapidly do so because they do not keep their mind in harmony. Conflicts, unresolved problems and worries cut-away life and subtract years very quickly. Poise and mental serenity keep our youthfulness and tends to rejuvenate, energize, and invigorate our body.

Look as though you were young. Dress in a style of today – with "the times." Throw back your shoulders and walk tall – with a bounce. You'll find your life will follow your posture! This works at any age, for health, confidence, and for attracting others.

> Don't give up on romance either. It will keep you youthful! Love, selflessness, kind-heartedness and goodwill keep the heart young.

Whenever you think of yourself, always hold the image of yourself as you would like to be. Don't focus on imperfections and weaknesses, because that will ruin your image, but hold resolutely to your ideal image and watch yourself come to resemble that image.

Recreation and play erase the effects of age better than any anti-wrinkle cream. Fun is youth's clone. Get out, go to a movie, take a vacation, do something you would never have done before.

Remember too that humor is one of the greatest destroyers and neutralizers of worry and misery. It increases circulation and promotes digestion. Happy people have a better night's sleep, more friends, and are less likely to be miserable or depressed. Studies show that lonely people die before those who have a wide social network. Sociability helps induce health and prolonged life. Dr. Patch Adams said "In my experience depression is not an illness it is a symptom, and the illness is loneliness." Consider spending time with children, they are always laughing – do you see the connection?

Growth is an opponent of age. The person who is always broadening their mind – learning, traveling, reading, discussing, keeping up with events – does not age nearly as rapidly as the one who has ceased to grow. Never stop reading; cancel your cable or satellite TV and get an Internet connection!

Someone who does not read is no better off then someone who cannot read.

Age accelerates when growing ends. Only dead things don't grow. When we allow our mind to stop expanding, to stop reaching, when our mind begins to grow dim on a diet of TV, when ambition halts, then death sets in. The mind begins to shut down, as do the muscles. Keep fit, keep reading, keep exploring, keep loving – and stay young.

The individual who feels the force of youth in their body, who holds clear, positive, youthful, confident thoughts, retains their youth. You are the captain of your financial ship and you control your health. We live in exciting, marvelous times, of great prosperity and wonder – stick around to see them!

A FINAL WORD

Financial Abundance is Waiting for You

Regardless of your financial status you *do* have the right to be prosperous. The power to be prosperous is not only within your grasp, it is actually within you now. Like an unused muscle, it's just waiting to be awakened and exercised. You already have the ability to achieve prosperity; you only need to learn how to stimulate it, to tap into the universe and claim it. There are methods you can use, steps you can take, and approaches you can make that will propel you toward abundance. This approach, called the 9 Cycles of Prosperity, will make you a magnet to prosperity. This book has provided you with the steps necessary to activate the Cycles.

Living the life of Cyclonic Wealth is not about financial tricks or "get-rich-quick" schemes. The key to your success is a mental process of change that you will go through as you adopt and use these methods to provide you with lasting wealth. As you follow the steps revealed in these pages, you'll discover how to achieve lasting prosperity!

Will Wealth Change You?

Some resist taking the step to prosperity because they feel wealth will change them in some negative way. This is false. Oprah Winfrey, one of television's wealthiest self-made celebrities, has said, "Though I am grateful for the blessings of wealth, it hasn't changed who I am. My feet are still on the ground. I'm just wearing better shoes." Oprah has taken her wealth and helped many people with it; she is an outstanding example of how money can do many things to benefit individuals and communities.

Wealth is only a result of the changes you will make to yourself, you will become better, smarter, and wiser; you will demonstrate leadership, intelligence and other fine qualities as you progress through the Cycles. As this happens, you will see your financial bottom line increase each day. Wealth will not "change" you – wealth is simply a result of the changes you will make to yourself.

Internalize the fact that you are right to desire to live a life of abundance. The famous American lawyer, writer and orator, Russell H. Conwell, makes your right to prosperity very clear in his book Acres of Diamonds. Conwell wrote:

> ... you ought to be rich; you have no right to be poor. To live and not be rich is a misfortune, and it is doubly a misfortune, because you could have been rich just as well as be poor ... You ought to be rich.

Money, income, and wealth are virtuous. The opposite is just as true: poverty is a sin; because of poverty, we have thieves and murderers in jails and at large, we have drunks, prostitutes and drug addicts on the streets and suicide rates are escalating.

Overwhelming poverty and large variances in the distribution of wealth were commonplace in most of history's communist regimes. These societies tried to eliminate private property by implementing a system in which goods were owned in common and expected to be available to all based on a prescribed level of need. The result was ruin, revolt and lingering alcoholism.

One could make an argument that 90% of the ills of mankind have been brought on because of poverty. However, taking money from the wealthy and handing it out to those who cherish poverty will not help; the answer to why that will not help is within these pages. Poverty is a state of mind. To change poverty, you must change the thought patterns of those who unknowingly embrace their poverty. We shall come to understand this better as we progress.

The Christian Bible is filled with rich promises regarding potential prosperity. In the scripture of Saint Matthew, we read from the Christ's *Sermon on the Mount*: "No one can serve two masters: for either he will hate the one, and love the other; or else he will hold to the one, and despise the other. Ye cannot serve God and mammon." From this we can see that success is not a master to be worshipped. Success is something to be achieved: it's not a god, it's a goal – a goal that each of us can reach. Success will not replace your beliefs and faith in a supreme being, it will augment it. Success can live harmoniously in your world as a measure of your achievements on earth and providing you with more time to dwell on spiritual or "higher" goals.

If you don't have money (i.e. mammon) it is your master and you are the follower. However, when you make money work for you, you are its master and the money follows you. This is the state you will achieve after putting this book into practice in your life. This is what we mean when we say "make money work for you," rather than "work for money."

Solomon realized the need to explore the rules of prosperity and gives clear guidance when saying "Poverty and shame shall be to him that refuseth instructions." In other words, those who reject education are condemned to poverty and shame; not those who are *uneducated*, but those who *reject* education. Today, we live in the Information Age and trade in a knowledge-based economy. With this reality, to reject education – information and knowledge – is the fastest way to poverty.

You may encounter some who despise wealth, and you may sense a certain degree of rejection from them as they see you change. Accept this. They will never know the joy of giving. They're likely only to dwell on how they can *take* from others – yet at the same time feel money is somewhat wrong, sinful, or even beneath them. Again, this thinking is not only false, but also dangerous to your soul, your life, and your future.

861730

Made in the USA